TRADE WAR

Containers Don't Lie, Navigating the Bluster

LORI ANN LAROCCO

Foreword by Arturo Sarukhan
Afterword by David M. Rubenstein

Marine Money, Inc.

Published by Marine Money, Inc.
100 First Stamford Place, 6th Floor
Stamford, Connecticut 06902
www.marinemoney.com

First Edition: November 2019

ISBN 13: 978-0-9978871-4-3 (Hardcover edition)
ISBN 13: 978-0-9978871-5-0 (Paperback edition)

To my mom,
Your words of encouragement and
guiding hand have created
the woman I am today.
Thank you for always opening
my eyes to what my tomorrow
could be and planting
the seeds of determination
that fuel my passion
for reporting the truth.
Love you

CONTENTS

FOREWORD

Begun, the trade wars have.

No one can claim to be surprised that President Donald Trump now has the makings of the trade war he's always wanted. We were all forewarned during the 2016 presidential campaign, when in his major foreign policy speech on April 27 in Washington, D.C., he reiterated that the world had grossly taken advantage of the United States, that he'd make it a less "predictable" nation on the world stage, and articulated his Sinatra Doctrine of "my way or the highway." As 2019 runs its course, President Trump has intensified his trade war with China, factories have been slowing down in major industrial nations, global commerce has been deteriorating rapidly, and the rules-based international trading system is badly frayed. All these trends rearing their heads represent perilous developments, threatening the world economy with a pronounced downturn. Trade policy today has turned into one of the most grievous geopolitical risks for the international community and for economies, businesses, and consumers everywhere, undermining the fairness, reciprocity, and level playing fields required to conduct equitable and beneficial trade around the world. If these trends continue, they will undoubtedly and irreparably damage the global and interconnected economy, sowing even more social and political discontent across different countries, dislocating more jobs, and feeding into authoritarianism and growing demagogic and chauvinistic populism, both on the right and on the left. History has certainly taught us the lesson of how that ends.

Few can deny that those economic and geopolitical dangers are unmistakable and mounting, threatening to spread from the factory floor to households and to polling booths in many major economies, particularly in the Americas, Europe, and Asia. The World Trade Organization has alerted that intensifying trade conflicts pose a dire and present danger to jobs and livelihoods across the globe, while discouraging companies from expanding and innovating. All the warning signs are clear enough: The trade war—and the weaponization of trade and trade policy by the current U.S. administration—along with the policy uncertainties about the future and the real and costly implementation and enforcement of trade restrictions—is wreaking worldwide havoc.

The telling trail of trade dislocation, pain, and danger is present everywhere. Both the United States and China—the world's two largest economies—have seen a pronounced cooling in commercial activity in recent months, a trend exacerbated by the tariffs they have imposed on each other's exports, raising costs for businesses and consumers, and discouraging investment. In Europe, trade is being stymied by fear that the United Kingdom may be on the verge of a tumultuous exit from the European Union, absent a deal governing future commerce across the English Channel and along the Ireland–Northern Ireland border. And tariffs and counter-tariffs, whether because of steel and aluminum or subsidies in the aerospace industries, are scuttling transatlantic ties. In North America, a revamped—though less than cutting-edge—free trade agreement among Canada, the U.S., and Mexico is still awaiting congressional ratification in Washington as the clock ticks down to a presidential election year that could basically doom United States–Mexico–Canada Agreement (USMCA) approval until after Election Day on November 3 of next year. Getting the revamped North American Free Trade Agreement (NAFTA) across the finish line on Capitol Hill was never going to be a walk in the park. NAFTA did indeed survive to fight another day, but North America lost a unique opportunity to truly modernize our trade flows and regulatory framework.

Beyond USMCA's positive impact on international financial markets and new and key provisions on digital flows, energy, stronger IP protection, e-commerce, and safeguards against government meddling in trade and financial services, some issues—such as the new rules of origin for the automotive sector—will continue to merit careful consideration. When President Trump rammed through the renegotiation of NAFTA, the three North American partners should have aimed for an ambitious and groundbreaking agreement to ensure that the USMCA delivered the new gold standard for international rules-based trade. Instead, we ended up with a ho-hum combination of new disciplines mixed with managed trade in the automotive sector. This has left some stakeholders with little incentives to push for congressional ratification beyond defending a framework similar to what we had in the past. Now, both timing and political calculations—and miscalculations—are conspiring to potentially complicate ratification further. Moreover, lurking in the foreground is Mr. Trump's ongoing threat of unilateral withdrawal from NAFTA if Congress does end up kicking the can down the road until after the U.S. presidential elections. And in the Pacific, the U.S. scored an own-goal by pulling out of the Trans-Pacific Partnership (TPP) among 12 Asian and American nations on the Pacific, one of the very first actions of the Trump Administration. U.S. participation, if not leadership, has been—and is—indispensable to international cooperation in areas like global trade. But Trump's isolationism now disrupts this paradigm. In many ways, the TPP—now the Comprehensive and Progressive Agreement for Trans-Pacific Partnership (or CPTPP) with the remaining 11 partners—was a coalition of the free-trade-willing, more about which nations wanted in to help build a 21st-century rules-based trading system. And withdrawing from the agreement denied U.S. exporters enhanced access to foreign markets, weakened North America's competitiveness as a whole across the Pacific, and was a gift to Chinese influence in Asia.

Additionally, parallel to these developments, the demands for new rules and disciplines governing the nexus of trade, investment, services, intellectual property, and business mobility are being increasingly formulated outside the World Trade Organization (WTO). Developing nations are rushing to unilaterally lower their tariffs (especially on intermediate goods) and reduce behind-the-border barriers to the trade-investment-services-IP nexus. Most nations continue to hammer out and sign bilateral investment treaties, and deeper regional trade agreements that provide them with the new, desperately needed disciplines for today's global economy. All of this has markedly eroded the WTO's centrality in the system of global trade governance.

President Trump's approach to trade seems to be based on a false understanding of how the global economy works, one that also plagued U.S. policy makers nearly a century ago. Essentially, the administration has forgotten an important lesson from the Great Depression. The most prominent trade war of the 20th century was ignited by the Smoot-Hawley Tariff act of 1930, which imposed steep tariffs on roughly 20,000 imported goods. Led by Canada, Washington's trading partners retaliated with tariffs on United States exports, which plunged 61 percent from 1929 to 1933. The tariffs were repealed in 1934. Historians and economists continue to debate the extent of the damage to the global economy, but there is little disagreement that Smoot-Hawley and the ensuing trade war exacerbated and prolonged the hardships of the Great Depression. Virtually all economists and trade researchers agree that the costs this time around could be as steep, and the still-preeminent position of the U.S. will not shield it—despite Oval Office rhetoric—from the dire consequences that unilateral trade policy can provoke.

Another parallel and truly troubling trend, as politicians and policy makers on both sides of the Atlantic and across the Pacific raise the stakes in the trade wars, mostly in tit-for-tat moves, trade is increasingly becoming a tool of coercion to achieve strategic influence, with the language and the narrative around trade also shifting. In the past, politicians and policy makers tended to describe trade as a mechanism for promoting global economic growth and well-being. Nowadays, statements about trade are steeped in a rhetoric of conflict. Instead of global opportunities, connectivity, wealth creation, and a rising tide lifting all boats, there's talk of protection, security, national interest, and defense. Former trade partners are now trade "enemies," with "unfair" protectionist policies against which it is natural—and only too tempting—for any politician to rail. Today, the international trade system that the U.S. helped to create, one based on open markets and classically liberal principles, is under threat as never before, and President Trump's "America First" approach is a total abdication of the traditional U.S. role as its defender, a policy that furthermore is, I would argue, dangerous not only for the U.S. economy but also for the international system. A Hobbesian approach to the world by the U.S.—still the most powerful nation in the world—will only guarantee Hobbesian reciprocity from other nations. It's a bad and worrisome combination indeed in what today is a very fluid international system.

A good crisis should never go to waste, and we need to step back from the brink before it's too late. Now's the time to rethink policy and approaches to global trade. In the current context of the trade wars, and the social and popular dissatisfaction with the benefits of global economic interconnectedness feeding the assault on trade policy, Lori Ann LaRocco's prescient book is a clarion call. LaRocco makes a compelling, timely, and well-documented case for the need to defend our trade flows, our joint production platforms and integrated supply chains, and the openness of our economies and, dare I say, our societies, but also explained and articulated to a skeptical and, in some cases, angry public. Politicians and government officials are not going to be willing to adopt serious solutions to the challenges we face in the coming years when their constituents have not been prepared to understand what the real options are, and when the scope for mistrust and retaliation is being unscrupulously fanned from the bully pulpits of leaders, politicians, and elected officials. Explaining the benefits of trade requires a delicate balance between economics and politics, and this book has found a persuasive way of doing so.

Ambassador Arturo Sarukhan *(former Mexican Ambassador to the United States, 2007–13)*

PREFACE

In a world where diplomacy and trade negotiations play out in real time on social media, it is understandable how the global markets could move so suddenly over a 280-character tweet. This is the first time in history that the world can be a spectator to this diplomatic process. Traditionally, negotiations have always occurred behind closed doors. The global audience was only made aware when a deal was done or broken off. There was a distinct separation between the ebbs and flows of deal-making. Those days are no more. Trade negotiations have become the world's number one business reality show. The delicate pendulum of fear and hope has been knocked off balance, which has sent the global markets on a ride of wild sell-offs and all-time highs.

President Donald Trump's red line for trade deals was laid out during the 2016 presidential election. Then Republican candidate Trump campaigned on being a leader who would follow through on his promises to "Make America Great Again" by using tariffs and renegotiating or withdrawing from "bad trade deals" to level the playing field for American businesses to compete. The marriage of economic vitality to national security was consummated. Unfair trade practices were deemed not only unfair but a national security threat.

This approach to negotiation should not come as a surprise. "Fair trade" was among Trump's rallying cries, and his belief in reciprocal trade precedes his presidency. In May 2014, then public citizen Trump tweeted for a crackdown on China's trade practices.

Donald J. Trump @
@realDonaldTrump

Remember, China is not a friend of the United States!

1:46 AM · May 20, 2014 · Twitter for Android

362 Retweets   **450** Likes

Just days after he formally announced that he would run for president, Trump tweeted a series of comments on the Trans-Pacific Partnership (TPP).[1] Twitter would become his favorite communication tool, a means of quickly getting his message out to the base.

On the campaign trail, Trump doubled down on TPP, calling the trade deal "another disaster done and pushed by special interests" and "a continuing rape of our country."[2] Just three days after assuming office, President Trump made good on his promise to withdraw from the partnership. In a memorandum, he explained that he would leave TPP and renegotiate with the countries one-on-one to get the best deal for America. "It is the policy of my Administration to represent the American people and their financial well-being in all negotiations, particularly the American worker, and to create fair and economically beneficial trade deals that serve their interests."[3] The administration set out on the path of bilateral negotiations, another promise Trump had made on the campaign trail.

In his Inaugural Address, President Trump laid out his plan to America, explaining that the foundation of his policies would meet the America First criteria. Interviews with the media further solidified his message regarding the need for fair trade deals and why tariffs would be an incentive for countries to come to the table. In his words, no longer would the United States be "disrespected, mocked, and ripped off."[4]

---

[1]   "The Trans-Pacific Partnership is an attack on America's business. It does not stop Japan's currency manipulation. This is a bad deal." —Donald J. Trump (@realDonaldTrump), April 22, 2015
"Republicans should not be giving Obama fast track authority on trade. The Trans-Pacific Partnership will squeeze our manufacturing sector." —Donald J. Trump (@realDonaldTrump), April 22, 2015
"The Trans-Pacific Partnership will lead to even greater unemployment. Do not pass it." —Donald J. Trump (@realDonaldTrump), April 22, 2015
"The Trans-Pacific Partnership is an attack on America's business. It does not stop Japan's currency manipulation. This is a bad deal." —Donald J. Trump (@realDonaldTrump), April 22, 2015
"China has a backdoor into the Trans-Pacific Partnership. This deal does not address currency manipulation. China is laughing at us." —Donald J. Trump (@realDonaldTrump), April 22, 2015

[2]   Cristiano Lima, "President Trump Calls Trade Deal 'a Rape of Our Country,'" Politico, June 28, 2016

[3]   "Presidential Memorandum Regarding Withdrawal of the United States From the Trans-Pacific Partnership Negotiations and Agreement," January 23, 2017

[4]   "Donald Trump Expounds on His Foreign Policy Views," edited transcript, The New York Times, June 3, 2016

The media and the rest of the world quickly learned that President Trump's Twitter account had replaced the traditional White House press release. He was the best messenger to expand on his policies, and he alone would inform the world on trade deal statuses, compromises, and dissatisfaction.

The multifront trade war, which started with solar panels and washing machines, quickly expanded to additional battles: the 232 action on aluminum and steel imports, intellectual property, automobiles, and immigration. As a result, retaliatory tariffs were imposed, and the flow of global trade that the world once knew was changed. Headlines reporting that the China tariffs were "on hold," "truces announced," as well as threats of additional tariffs being imposed, continue to feed the uncertainty, sending the markets to historic highs and dramatic sell-offs.

So how can one get a sense of the true status of trade and the good faith being pledged by countries like China? Through the trade flows. The containers, cargo, LNG, and oil that travel on these ocean highways tell you what is truly happening. Promises and rhetoric are just words. The status of trade talks and whether the United States is "winning" can be revealed by the movement of trade.

In this book you will read a real-time chronology of the multiple-front trade wars, but more importantly you will see data of the containers and cargo. The data provides the unvarnished, unbiased reality of the trade war. The flow allows you to see the cause and effect of tariffs. Just like the old saying "sunlight is the best disinfectant," the flow of trade provides the necessary transparency to reveal the reality of trade.

With 90 percent of the world's economy moved by maritime transport, the ocean highway is the best way for anyone to monitor the flow of trade and gauge the status of trade talks. Remember the two phrases your parents told you when you were a teen—"Talk is cheap" and "Actions speak louder than words"? Well, when it comes to the world of shipping, action is being taken. Containers and tankers don't lie. Let's cut through the political rhetoric and see what the tea leaves of maritime are telling us, and the strategies some business leaders are employing to navigate the trade wars.

PROLOGUE

The United States' desire to expand its trade routes with China dates back to the 1800s. At the end of that century, the United States proposed the Open Door Policy, asking for "fair field and no favor," an opportunity for China to trade with all nations equally.

Source: Niday Picture Library/Alamy Stock Photo

The term was used again in 1978 when Deng Xiaoping, then paramount leader of the People's Republic of China, opened the country for foreign direct investment. U.S.-China trade relations were formally established in 1979 when U.S. President Jimmy Carter acknowledged mainland China's One China principle and granted full diplomatic recognition that Taiwan was an official part of China.[5] President Bill Clinton later expanded trade relations with the signing of the U.S.-China Relations Act of 2000. This paved the way for China to join the World Trade Organization (WTO) in 2001. The United States supported China's joining the WTO as a way of combating the non-tariff barriers and trade-distorting practices of China, more commonly known as currency manipulation.

To review the national security implications of trade and economic ties between the United States and China, the U.S.-China Security Review Commission

---

[5]   One-China policy is the policy saying Taiwan is part of China.

(USCC) was created by the U.S. Congress on October 30, 2000. It's first report was issued on July 15, 2002. With the benefit of hindsight, it's eye-opening to see how the U.S. concerns and trade conflicts with China really have not changed. The only difference today is the larger trade deficit.

In its inaugural report, the USCC wrote: "The United States has played a major role in China's rise as an economic power. Fueled by China's virtually inexhaustible supply of low-cost labor and large inflows of foreign direct investment (FDI), the U.S. trade deficit with China has grown at a furious pace—from $11.5 billion in 1990 to $85 billion in 2000. The U.S. trade deficit with China is not only our largest deficit in absolute terms but also the most unbalanced trading relationship the U.S. maintains."[6] Morgan Stanley's report that same year referred to the U.S. deficit with China as "nothing short of staggering."[7]

Figure 2.1
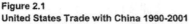
United States Trade with China 1990-2001

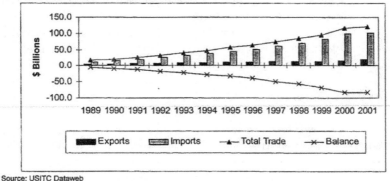

Source: USITC Dataweb

FDIs in labor-intensive industries drove Chinese exports to new highs as manufacturers migrated to China for low-cost labor. This "investment" overseas actually took a bite out of U.S. labor. The $10 billion 2006 investment made by Motorola (which at the time was the largest exporter among China's foreign-invested firms) lead to the reduction of employment at the company's U.S. facilities. This movement of money drove U.S. imports from China even higher and permanently shifted the trading patterns between the U.S. and Asia.

---

6   U.S.-China Security Review Commission, Report to Congress, Executive Summary, October 30, 2000, 4

7   Joseph P. Quinlan, "America's Trade Deficit With China: Why It's Here to Stay," Morgan Stanley Equity Research, Special Economic Study, March 22, 2002, 7

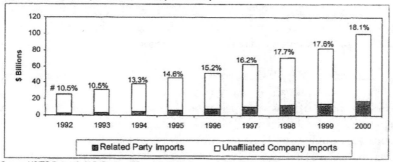

Figure 2.4 — U.S. Imports from China (1992-2000)

Source: USITC Dataweb, U.S. Bureau of Economic Analysis; compiled by USCC Staff
Percentage of Imports due to Related Party Trade

While China's accession into the WTO was supported by the world's major trading partners, the George W. Bush administration explained that China's WTO membership would not reduce the ballooning U.S. trade deficit with China. In testimony before the USCC, then Assistant Secretary of Commerce William Lash said, "The WTO was not designed to address the trade deficit; it was designed to increase our market access and to increase, frankly, a level playing field with rule of law so that our exporters and our workers can get a fair deal when trying to export to the Chinese market."[8]

Technology Transfers

In 2001, 124 high-tech research and development (R&D) centers were operating by U.S. majority-owned foreign firms and working jointly with Chinese state-controlled universities and firms. According to the USCC, technology transfers were commonly used as dealmakers by U.S. firms looking to ink joint R&D contracts with Chinese institutions and labs once U.S. companies had access to China. Before agreeing with the WTO obligations, China had to cease such practices. Citing a State Department report to Congress on U.S. Science and Technology Corporation, the USCC wrote, "'This Chinese investment strategy, designed to extract technology transfer from American firms as a condition for entering the Chinese market, is, in State's estimation, the principal source of technology transfer from the U.S. to China.'... [China]

---

8   U.S.-China Security Review Commission, "WTO Compliance and Sectoral Issues, Oral Testimony of William H. Lash, II," January 18, 2002, 55

'reaps a technology bonanza' from these investment policies. And, this trend will most likely continue, if not accelerate."[9]

In its report "U.S. Commercial Technology Transfers to the People's Republic of China," the Department of Commerce wrote, "it is clear that foreign firms are being coerced into transferring technology (which they probably would not otherwise do) as the price to be paid for access to China's market."

In 2001, the American Chamber of Commerce in China (AmCham-China) also voiced its concern. "Despite the updating of provisional regulations on technology licensing in preparation for China's WTO entry, foreign companies are still required to submit technology licensing documents to the Chinese government for review—and licensors often must trade significant technology rights for approval to continue their project. In some industries informal administrative measures in the form of 'advice' to foreign companies make technology transfer a precondition of market entry. AmCham-China strongly believes China needs to take a more progressive and open approach to end such irregular practices."[10]

The USCC concluded that policing IP theft would be difficult and China's broad commitments to eliminate its discriminatory and trade-distorting practices would have the potential to significantly enhance market access for U.S. goods and services.

China's View on Global Trade

China formally entered the WTO on December 11, 2001. The People's Daily, the Communist Party's official news outlet, laid out the goals of China as a WTO member. These bullets provide keen insight into China's view on trade today:

- *We should make full use of the favorable conditions offered by entry into the WTO, implement diversified strategies and try by every possible means to enlarge exports. While guaranteeing maintenance of our traditional export markets, we should actively explore new export markets and vigorously advance the diversity of markets.*

---

9   U.S.-China Security Review Commission, "Hearing on Export Controls and China, Written Testimony of Bernard D. Cole and Paul H.B. Goodwin," January 17, 2002, 3

10   American Chamber of Commerce-China, "American Business in China: 2001 White Paper," February 2001, 60

- *We should strengthen energy resource cooperation with foreign countries and gradually realize the diversification of channels for the import of important strategic materials.*
- *We should actively spur foreign capital to flow into high and new technological industries and encourage transnational corporations to come to China to set up R&D centers and regional headquarters.*

Rapid Ascent

Between 1980 and 2004, trade between the U.S. and China increased from $5 billion to $231 billion. China became the sweet spot for foreign direct investment, knocking Mexico out of the top slot. Mexico had been the number one destination for FDI because of NAFTA.[11] Joseph Quinlan noted in his report that the low-cost manufacturing platform China provided was the best way to compete in the global marketplace. "China's massive consumer and labor markets do set it apart from the rest of the world, and for many U.S. firms, there is simply no choice but to be on the ground there."

In addition to investment, China surpassed Mexico as the United States' second largest trading partner in 2006. The interdependence between the United States and China grew. In September 2008, China became the largest holder of U.S. debt (treasuries), at approximately $600 billion.

One Belt, One Road Initiative

In September and October 2013, Xi Jinping, China's paramount leader, unveiled an initiative originally called the One Belt, One Road initiative during his visits to Kazakhstan and Indonesia. The plan would build up and enhance China's geopolitical influence around the world by developing infrastructure partnerships with more than 60 countries across Asia, Africa, Europe, and Latin America. In 2016, the name of the plan was changed to the Belt Road Initiative (BRI). The BRI would connect China to international markets with three roads, a maritime route, the e-Silk Road, and the String of Pearls.

The first of the three roads covered the ancient Silk Road, running from China to Rome. The northern branch connected China to Russia, and the southernmost branch connected China to Europe through Iran. Together, these routes passed through Asia and North Africa, connecting East Asia with Europe and Russia.

---

[11] Quinlan, "America's Trade Deficit With China," 3

The maritime route linked China's seas with the Mediterranean, Indian Ocean, Arabian Sea, and Red Sea. The e-Silk Road was a digitally linked road connecting regions and countries that wanted to trade with China. The String of Pearls referred to the strategy of acquiring valuable ports that can connect to strategic maritime trade routes (for example, the Piraeus port in Athens). In the end, the main goal of this trading strategy was to open China to the world and diversify its export and import markets.

Bruce Jones, vice president and director of foreign policy at the Brookings Institution, described the BRI as "a leading indicator of the scale of China's global ambitions."[12] Since 2013, more than 130 countries have signed deals or expressed interest in projects along the Silk Road. The World Bank has estimated that $575 billion in projects are being constructed. But the BRI has a long way to go. "Challenges include infrastructure and policy gaps in the BRI corridor economies, foreign investment, and debt and government risks that would slow down trade."[13] According to Refinitiv, the total value of projects is around $3.67 trillion.

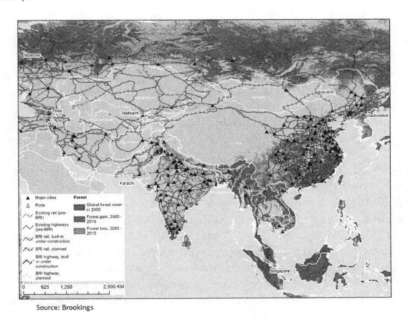

Source: Brookings

12   Fred Dews, "Charts of the Week: China's Belt and Road Initiative," Brookings Now, May 17, 2019
13   "Belt and Road Economics: Opportunities and Risks of Transport Corridors," World Bank Group, June 18, 2019

The goal of the BRI was based on Xi's plan of sustainability and creating diverse opportunity. Not relying on a single country for trade was an essential piece of China's trade philosophy. Having a variety of trading partners for a single commodity was part of Xi's plan.

Subsidies and Dumping

For decades, China has used large quantities of subsidies as a way of growing its state-owned enterprises (SOE). This reliance on subsidies is not new, and the United States and other countries have filed with the WTO their grievances regarding the unfair advantages these subsidies have had in the global marketplace.

Unlike capitalism, which encourages competition based on success through innovation without government assistance, subsidies are considered anti-competitive behavior and harmful to the overall economy. Instead of companies gaining market share through commercial competition, a subsidized business environment is driven by government intervention. Subsidies can be offered in the forms of financial assistance and regulatory measures.

The United States has argued that the subsidies offered by the Chinese government have enabled these SOEs to grow and produce at such a rate that they monopolize the market share and, in effect, artificially lower the price of the product with the sheer volume of product flooding into the market. Since the price point to produce the product is lower for Chinese companies because of the subsidies, they can afford the lower sales price. Competitors cannot.

The amount of subsidies can be tracked as "loans" on the bank sheets of China's People's Bank. According to the testimony of Derek Scissors, resident scholar of the American Enterprise Institute before the Senate Banking Committee, "At the end of 2012, the People's Bank reported outstanding loan volume of $12.93 trillion. On the order of $10.3 trillion was loaned to SOEs, and almost all of that on noncommercial terms—at near-zero costs or with optional repayment. This certainly does not constitute a $10 trillion subsidy, since there would be a large amount of lending under a commercial banking system. But the amount of capital affected by Chinese subsidies and used by SOEs is approximately $10 trillion."[14]

---

[14] Derek Scissors, "Testimony before the Senate Committee on Banking, Housing, and Urban Affairs Subcommittee on Economic Policy," December 11, 2013

According to the corporate earnings data collected and analyzed by the financial database Wind, payments by Beijing and local governments to the 3,545 listed companies rose 14 percent year-over-year to $22.3 billion in 2018. The data did not include private companies, which account for the majority of the Chinese economy. Jiang Chao, an analyst at brokerage Haitong Securities, estimated the total value of subsidies to the corporate sector in 2017 was 430 billion yuan or about $6.7 billion.

Sector Chinese Government Subsidies

Table 1: Where Public Ownership Still Dominates	
Alternative energy and energy conservation	Materials
Autos	Media
Aviation	Metals
Banking	Oil and gas
Biologic science	Petrochemicals
Coal	Power
Construction	Railways
Environmental Protection	Securities
Information technology	Shipping
Insurance	Telecom
Machinery	Tobacco

Source: American Enterprise Institute, Derek

The use of subsidies by countries is not uncommon. The United States offers subsidies for farming, oil, ethanol, housing, Obamacare, and other industries that the government deems important to help fuel the U.S. economy.[15] Remember Cash for Clunkers in 2009?[16]

U.S. subsidies also include multibillion-dollar tax breaks to domestic companies. According to OpenTheBooks Oversight Report, federal funding of Fortune 100 companies in the fiscal year 2014 through fiscal year 2018 received $392 billion in federal contract procurement and $3.2 billion in federal grants.

---

[15] Subsidies via the Department of Agriculture (USDA), Department of Energy (DOE), DOE, Department of Housing and Urban Development (HUD), respectively.

[16] Cash for Clunkers was a program designed to spark auto sales. It encouraged people to buy more fuel-efficient cars by offering a $3,500–$4,500 rebate. Dealers would receive a subsidy of up to $4,500 from the U.S. government after discounting a new vehicle to a buyer who traded in an old vehicle.

But no subsidies can compare to the deep and vast pocketbook of China. In 2016, a total of 41 investigations were launched over Chinese steel products by 16 countries and regions. The number of complaints was up 24 percent year-over-year, according to China's government data. China denied it had engaged in dumping and said that the global steel overcapacity was caused by a shortage of worldwide demand, not excessive supply.[17]

Projected Annual Cost of Energy-Related Tax Incentives: FY1978-FY2022

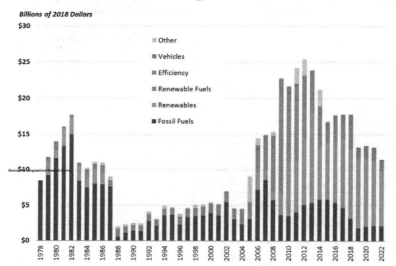

Source: CRS, using data from the Joint Committee on Taxation and Office of Management and Budget

The enormous volumes of China exports being dumped into the global markets hit foreign competition hard. As the complaints to the WTO grew and countervailing duties were imposed on China, the country eventually started to expand and boost production around the world with overseas investments. These overseas companies would receive capital from Chinese state-owned funds and lenders.

Reducing the amount of subsidies has been a key point in the trade talks between China and the United States. Despite the promises of reducing the amount of subsidies, the fight has continued. The U.S. Trade Representative (USTR) Robert Lighthizer said China has failed to disclose its subsidies as required by the WTO and presented a catalog of 500 different subsidies and

---

17   "China Files WTO Complaint Against U.S., E.U. Over Price Comparison Methodologies," dispute settlement, December 12, 2016, wto.org

supports, including access to capital and land. The size of China's subsidy program for local government is largely unknown. According to reporting by Reuters, when the Chinese negotiators were asked, they said they did not know the details of all of the programs.[18]

U.S. Imports, Exports, and the Trade Deficit with China, January 2018–July 2019

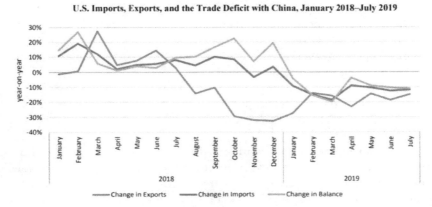

Source: U.S. Census Bureau, *Trade in Goods with China*, September 4, 2019. https://www.census.gov/foreign-trade/balance/c5700.html.
U.S.-China Economic and Security Review Commission

"China continues to shield massive subcentral government subsidies from the scrutiny of WTO members," the USTR said in a February 2019 report to Congress on China's WTO compliance.

China 2025

In May 2015, the China State Council unveiled another plan for boosting its sustainability. It was called Made in China 2025. The 35-page action plan focused on transforming the country's manufacturing sector from the "world's factory" for cheap, low-quality goods into a producer of higher-value services and products such as manufacturing in fields like information technology (IT), robotics, and semiconductors. This proposal was part of China's strategy to transform the country into a "manufacturing power" by the year 2049, the 100th anniversary of the People's Republic of China.

Nine tasks were laid out as priorities to achieve this goal: enhancing manufacturing innovation, better utilization of technology and industry, strengthening the industrial base, creating fostering Chinese brands, promoting

---

[18] "U.S. Is Said to Water Down Demand That China Curb Subsidies Amid Push for a Trade Deal," Reuters, April 14, 2019

the development and use of green manufacturing, and developing breakthroughs in 10 key sectors. The 10 sectors were:

1. New information technology
2. High-end numerically controlled machine tools and robots
3. Aerospace equipment
4. Ocean engineering equipment and high-end vessels
5. High-end rail transportation equipment
6. Energy-saving cars and new energy cars
7. Electrical equipment
8. Farming machines
9. New materials, such as polymers.
10. Bio-medicine and high-end medical equipment

China would also encourage further advancement of its markets and attract foreign investors in the areas of new information technology and bio-medicine. The establishment of R&D centered around foreign companies and institutions would also be encouraged. This plan sparked international criticism on the massive use of subsidies as well as the policies that required technology transfer as a condition for doing business in China.[19]

IP Theft and Tech Transfer Battle Heats Up

Just 10 days before President Trump and Xi's December trade meeting, USTR Lighthizer filed a report accusing China of continuing to steal intellectual property and technology. According to BSA, the Software Alliance, approximately 66 percent of the software that is used in China, valued at $6.8 billion, is pirated.[20]

The Council on Foreign Relations said that many of China's means of acquiring IP are not officially written into law but are done in indirect and informal ways that make it difficult to prosecute.[21] In written testimony to the USTR about the theft of American intellectual property, the IP Commission said, "Through means such as investments and cyber intrusion, the Chinese government directs and unfairly facilitates the systematic acquisition of cutting-edge technologies in industries deemed important by state industrial plans. The report concludes that

---

[19] "Made in China 2025: Global Ambitions Built on Local Protection," U.S. Chamber of Commerce, America, Chamber of Commerce in China, January 16, 2019
[20] "BSA Global Software Survey in Brief," BSA, the Software Alliance, June 2018
[21] James McBride and Andrew Chatzky, "Is 'Made in China 2025' a Threat to Global Trade?" Council on Foreign Relations, May 13, 2019

China's acts, policies, and practices are unreasonable because they unfairly target critical U.S. technology with the goal of achieving dominance in strategic sectors. These practices harm U.S. innovation and economic competitiveness."[22]

The IP Commission estimated that "the scale of the annual theft of American IP likely surpasses the U.S. trade deficit with China; in 2017 the goods trade deficit was $375 billion, while in comparison, the loss of American IP likely reaches $600 billion annually."[23] Eighty-seven percent of the counterfeit goods seized at the U.S. port of entry are sourced from China.

Ballooning Trade Deficit

President Trump pledged that his trade strategy over the long term would "rebalance the global economy" through the imposing of tariffs for national security reasons, pursuing and inking new trade deals with strategic partners, and firmly enforcing U.S. trade laws. Since the trade war started, America's deficit with China reached $87 billion in the second quarter of 2019.[24]

Because of China's reciprocal tariff actions, U.S. exports to China have dropped precipitously. Exports were down 22.4 percent in the first six months of 2019 nationwide compared to the same time frame in 2018. Exports for the full year of 2018 were down 3.87 percent.[25] In the second quarter, the contraction in trade contributed to a decrease in the U.S. trade deficit with China. U.S. exports to China were down 18.7 percent year-over-year ($26 billion), and U.S. imports totaled $113 billion (down 10.7 percent year-over-year).[26] In the first six months of 2019, the U.S. goods trade deficit with China was $167 billion, down 10.1 percent from the same period in 2018.[27]

---

[22] "IP Commission 2019 Review: Progress and Updated Recommendations," IP Commission, February 2019, 3

[23] "Section 301 Investigation: China's Acts, Policies, and Practices Related to Technology Transfer, Intellectual Property, and Innovation," Docket No.: USTR-2018-0005-0001, IP Commission, May 11, 2018, 3

[24] "Economics and Trade Bulletin," U.S.-China Economic and Security Review Commission, August 5, 2019

[25] Port of Los Angeles, PIERS, IHS Markit

[26] "Economics and Trade Bulletin," USCC, August 5, 2019

[27] "Economics and Trade Bulletin," USCC, August 5, 2019

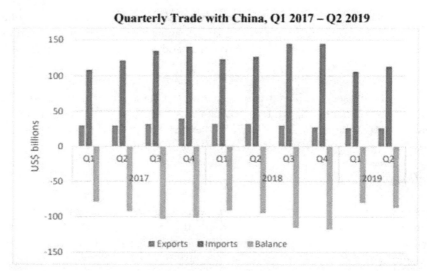

Quarterly Trade with China, Q1 2017 – Q2 2019

Source: U.S. Census Bureau, Trade in Goods with China, August 5, 2019
https://www.census.gov/foreign-trade/balance/c5700.html

China's deceleration of growth continued in the second quarter of 2019, posting a growth rate of 6.2 percent, down slightly from 6.4 percent in the first quarter. It was the slowest growth rate recorded since China began publishing quarterly data in 1992. U.S.-China trade tensions, Beijing's deleveraging campaign, and weak domestic demand all contributed to the decline. To help inject vibrancy back into its economy, the government deployed significant stimulus measures. Starting in December 2018, $190 billion in new infrastructure spending and $170 billion in cuts to business taxes and fees were introduced. According to the USCC, the stimulus helped stall sharper deceleration but did not halt the slowdown.

Fixed-asset investment (FAI) and industrial output helped fuel the first quarter thanks to the subsidiaries. Investment in buildings, machinery, and equipment rose 5.8 percent in the first half of 2019, down slightly from 6 percent in 2018.

Industrial output grew 6 percent in the first half of the year, compared with 6.2 percent in 2018. Retail sales grew 8.4 percent in the first half of 2019, a little lower than the 9 percent growth seen a year earlier. In June of 2019, retail sales surged to a 16-month high of 9.8 percent driven almost entirely by auto sales. Chinese dealers offered steep discounts to offload inventory that did not meet the new emission standards that were taking effect on July 1.

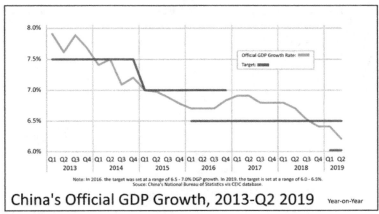

Graph: Marine Money International

Despite the slowing down of its economy, over the course of the trade war China has remained undeterred in its mission of growing, expanding its well of trading partners, and adding alternative sellers for U.S. exports like crude oil, LNG, and agriculture products through its BRI trading partners. The U.S. bucket of imports was being filled by other countries.

Meanwhile, if the United States wanted to make up for the loss of soybean trade with China, it would need to have a 92 percent market share with every country importing U.S. soybeans.[28] That is a market share the United States does not have.

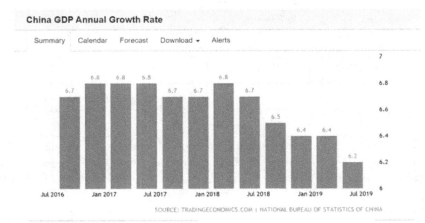

Source: Trading Economics

---

28   Dale Hildebrant, "Expanding Soybean Export Markets," Farm and Ranch Guide, August 16, 2019

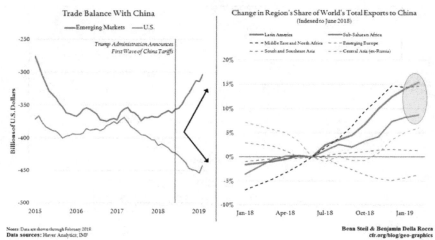

Source: CFR.org. Reprinted with permission. Benn Steil and Benjamin Della Rocca, "Trump's Trade War Puts 'Belt and Road First,'" Geo-Graphics (blog), August 12, 2019, http://cfr.org/blog/trumps-trade-war-puts-belt-and-road-first

The trade war comes at a crucial economic time for China. The country is facing three large economic problems: high government debt, the imbalance between the public and private sectors, and the transitioning of the country's economy from one that was powered by the manufacturing sector to an economy led by consumers.

At the annual National People's Congress, Chinese Premier Li Keqiang announced in his opening remarks that the Chinese government budget deficit in 2019 was expected to widen to 2.76 trillion yuan, representing around 2.8 percent of the country's gross domestic product.[29] The high debt is having an impact on the efficiencies between the country's public and private sectors. The public sector has better access to bank loans and government subsidies, which leaves private companies at a greater risk for liquidity crunches as the country tries to reign in their debt.

China's consumer-driven economy has faced a series of headwinds in 2019. Mother Nature and the trade war have created a cocktail of inflation that has world economists concerned. According to the National Bureau of Statistics, July food prices soared 9.1 percent from a year ago after the country was hit with severe weather hurting the country's fruit supply and swine fever decimated its pork population.

---

[29]   Li Keqiang, "Report on the Work of the Government," The State Council, the People's Republic of China, updated March 16, 2019

The interconnectedness of the global economies exposes countries to both prosperity and slowdowns. Like a puzzle, each country is a vital piece to the overall picture. Without one, it is not complete. Export growth is the glue that binds the countries together. That growth thrives on the producers and consumers of the world. Trade tensions have been shown to negatively impact both.[30]

The ripple effects created by the reduction of trade between the U.S. and China have stained both the global business and financial market sentiment. The International Monetary Fund (IMF) has been warning for months about the negative impact the trade war could have on the global economy. Just hours after China retaliated with its own set of tariffs in response to tariffs to be levied on September 1, 2019, Federal Reserve Chief Jerome Powell spoke about the consequences of the trade war at the annual monetary conference at Jackson Hole, Wyoming: "Trade policy uncertainty seems to be playing a role in the global slowdown and in weak manufacturing and capital spending in the United States."

The rhetoric of tweets and fiery statements may consume the world stage, stirring the crippling emotions of fear and anxiety, but the truth does not reside there. The reality in this historic trade war is in the flow of trade. The containers, cargo, and tankers that the global ports welcome every day provide the insight needed to gauge the health of a country's economy, and the business of trade itself.

It's time now to peel away the bluster of words and reveal the trade war's true story, which only maritime can tell.

---

[30] Eugenio Cerutti, Gita Gopinath, Adil Mohommad, "The Impact of U.S.-China Trade Tensions," IMF Blog, International Monetary Fund, May 23, 2019

CHAPTER ONE

Trade Flows

At any given moment, more than 50,000 vessels are traveling on the water superhighway transporting global trade. Marine Traffic, a website that tracks the vessels via their GPS transponders, shows a live map like the one below for those who are monitoring incoming vessels. It's an impressive and over-whelming sight to see.

Over the past century, the amount of trade being transported by the shipping industry has more than quadrupled. What was behind this amazing growth? Free trade. How is that measured? By the number of containers, cargo, and commodities delivered into ports around the world.

There is a direct correlation between the growth of global trade and the expansion of ports around the world. The volume of trade provides the tea leaves that tell the story of the health of a country's economy based on its imports and exports, and show the relationship a country has with its trading partners. In the United States, the ports of Los Angeles, Long Beach, and New York and New Jersey are among the top 25 container ports in the world.[31]

---

[31]   Los Angeles ranked 17, Long Beach ranked 21, and New York and New Jersey ranked 24. "Top 50 global port rankings 2018," JOC.com, August 9, 2019

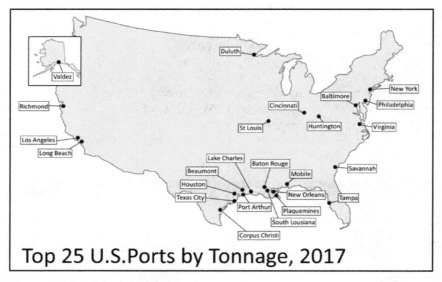

Top 25 U.S.Ports by Tonnage, 2017

Source: Marine Money International

Since the end of World War II, more than 500 bilateral and regional trade agreements have been signed, including the two major global multilateral deals: the General Agreement on Tariffs and Trade (GATT), and the treaty that established the World Trade Organization (which replaced GATT in 1995). These trade agreements, along with advances in technology, industrialization, the liberalization of national economies, and globalization, have not only buoyed world trade but created an economic interconnectedness. Economist Richard Baldwin once said: "Regional trade liberalization sweeps the globe like wildfire."

As in all sectors, the maritime industry directly benefits from a vibrant, growing, global economy. If trading partners are in an economic expansion, the demand for goods is greater. If a major trading partner starts to slow, or if there is an economic disruption, that kind of shock sparks fears of a global contagion, and demand diminishes.

For a visual reference of world trade, think of the flow of goods and commodities as a complex network of plumbing. Trade agreements are the pipe adaptors, which help expand trade. Tariffs, on the other hand, can act as either a stopper, blocking the flow of trade into a specific country, or an elbow pipe, diverting the flow away from one country to another.

The true story behind the trade war begins and ends at the ports. U.S. exports are a shining example of the failure of the trade talks. Words expressed in a trade war are meaningless if there is no action behind them. Also, the positive rhetoric must be put into perspective. There have been multiple headlines about China buying soybeans. That is merely a distraction. China was buying agriculture products before the war even began, and based on the data, the United States is in the hole.

For example, one of the biggest phenomena to result from the U.S. trade war with its trading partners has been the acceleration of production and shipment to avoid upcoming tariff increases. This front-loading of orders creates an artificial export surge into U.S. ports. Since the first round of tariffs on Chinese imports were imposed in early July 2018, U.S. ports on the West Coast have reported historic volumes of product.

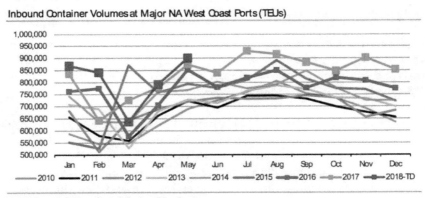

Inbound Container Volumes at Major NA West Coast Ports (TEUs)

Includes the ports of LA, Long Beach, Oakland, and Prince Rupert.

Sources: Port Authorities, SFG Research FreightWaves

"The volumes at the port tell the story of the tariffs," explained Gene Seroka, executive director of the Port of Los Angeles. "We saw rises in volume just ahead of tariff announcement dates, and then on the export side we were down every single month in calendar year 2018. Every single month U.S. exports to China were down. Our best month was down 9 percent; our worst month was at the end of the year, down 45 percent year-over-year." The Port of Los Angeles is the largest port in the United States and the busiest container port in North America.

The Trump Trade Narrative Laid Out

The sweeping blueprint of the U.S. trade war was laid out on March 1, 2017, when U.S. Trade Representative (USTR) Robert Lighthizer released President Trump's 2017 Trade Policy Agenda. The report outlined the new administration's four fair trade priorities: promoting U.S. sovereignty, enforcing U.S. trade laws, leveraging U.S. economic strength to expand our goods and services exports, and protecting U.S. intellectual property rights.

On his 100th day in office, April 29, 2017, President Trump directed both the USTR and the Department of Commerce to submit, within 180 days, a report reviewing the performance of current trade agreements, identifying trade abuses, and offering trade remedies. Secretary of State Rex Tillerson, Treasury Secretary Steven Mnuchin, Attorney General Jeff Sessions, and Director of the Office of Trade and Manufacturing Policy Peter Navarro also worked on this extensive review.

Based on the recommendations of Commerce Secretary Wilbur Ross and Lighthizer, President Trump approved the imposing of tariffs on both solar panels and washing machines as part of his America First agenda on January 22, 2018. The first shot of the trade war was fired.

Lighthizer explained there would be a tariff of 20 percent on the first 1.2 million washers, and in the following two years a 50 percent tariff on all subsequent imported washers. A 30 percent tariff would be imposed on solar panel components, with the rate declining over four years. China criticized the trade move, saying it was wrong to take unilateral action and that the move could threaten the international trading system.

As a matter of order, when a tariff action is announced, there is a public comment period, set by the USTR, during which companies can submit their support or concern for the trade measure to the Federal Register. They can also testify in public hearings. It was during the public comment period that companies started to ramp up their export of solar panels and washing machines in order to avoid possible tariffs. This is called front-loading. According to these targeted products' bills of lading, which detail what is in a container as well as its country of origin, destination, and client in order to allow a company to keep track of its product throughout the transport process, between September 1 and December 31, 2017, 4,233 containers holding solar panels were imported to the United States. Once the tariffs were officially imposed, the number of containers imported dropped drastically, to 1,734 containers between January 1 and April 30, 2018. Washing machines saw a similar pattern of front-loading: 3,477 containers filled with washing machines from China were imported between September 1 and December 31, 2017; when the tariff was imposed, the number dropped to 1,887 containers over the first three months of 2018.

"1.3 million washing machines were imported into the United States ahead of the tariff," Steve Ferreira, CEO of Ocean Audit, said. "They avoided $162 million in tariffs. After the tariffs were imposed, the imports of washing machines dropped to 516,000 units."

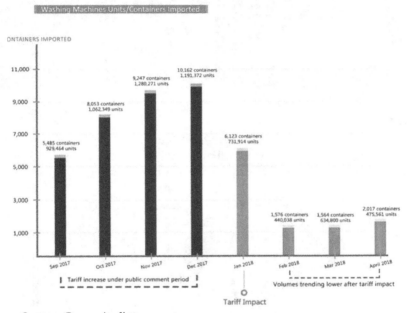

Source: Ocean Audit

Retailers could not wait to see if the tariffs would be imposed. The risk of waiting was too great, and the window to transport their products to the United States was small. Transport by sea from China to the United States is not quick. Shipment arrivals can vary depending on delivery service purchased. Shipment's from China can take 15 to 20 days to reach the U.S. West Coast and approximately 33 to 35 days to reach the East Coast. And these are just the open-water travel dates; they do not include the planning, transport of product from the manufacturers, supply houses, and loading of the containers onto the ship.

The flow of trade from China to the United States surged with the front-loading. The tremendous volumes were headlines in the news.

Monthly retail imports 2018-2019
(TEU - Millions)

NRF RETAIL

But not being noticed was the disturbing trend of the continuous drop in U.S. exports to China and other countries as a result of counter tariffs.

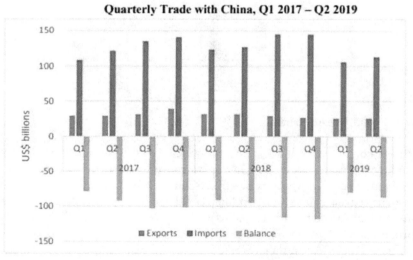

Quarterly Trade with China, Q1 2017 – Q2 2019

Source: U.S. Census Bureau, Trade in Goods with China, August 5, 2019
https://www.census.gov/foreign-trade/balance/c5700.html

These retaliatory tariffs came at the hand of trading partners that were included in the United States' tariffs on solar panels and washing machines, as well as U.S. tariffs on steel and aluminum imports into the United States. From the European Union's tariffs on whiskey, navy beans, and motorcycles to India's tariffs on almonds and apples to the agriculture and recycling counter tariffs from China, the United States saw a series of plugs inserted into the flow of trade. Some markets were simply wiped out with the stroke of a pen.

"Our European buyers told us they wanted to put all shipments on hold until the trade talks get settled out," said Tom Lix, CEO of Cleveland Whiskey. "Once the tariff was official, shipments were then canceled. The E.U. made up 15 percent of our overall revenue. Now it's gone."

Farming Industry Frayed by Trade War

Out of all the U.S. industries targeted by these retaliatory tariffs, the impact on the American farmer has perhaps been the most widely reported. The Chinese retaliatory tariffs on soybeans, corn, pork, and poultry, and the subsequent increase in the buying of Brazilian soybeans, are good examples of the diversion in the flow of trade.

This map from the United States Department of Agriculture (USDA) shows the flow of the soybean trade before the trade war.

Leading soybean exporters and destinations during 2016/17

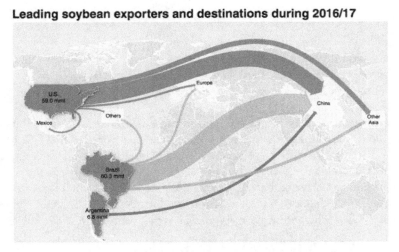

Note: Chart shows production of soybeans by United States, Brazil, and Argentina during 2016/17. Width of arrows represents volume of exports. mmt = million metric tons.

Source: ERS analysis of customs data from IHS Global Insight, Global Trade Atlas.

Source: USDA, Report from the Economic Research Service, June 2019

Today, as can be seen in the chart below, U.S. soybean exports to China have been eviscerated. The tariffs with the Chinese have halted U.S. soybean exports and increased Brazilian soybean exports. Despite the trade negotiations, while China has purchased soybeans over the course of the trade war, those purchases do not compare to the historical volumes.

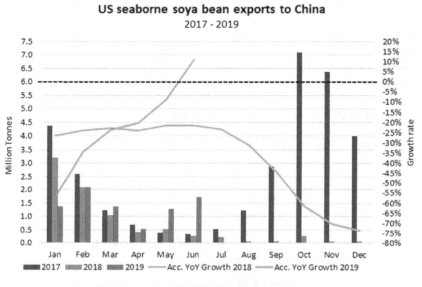

US seaborne soya bean exports to China
2017 - 2019

Source: BIMCO, US Census Bureau

During a typical year, one third of the U.S. soybean crop is sold to China. As a rule, farmers can make forward sales (contracts) at any time of the year when they feel the price of the crop is at a desired level.

"The farmers have taken it on the chin in these negotiations," said Christopher Gibbs, a farmer and former county executive director for the USDA Farm Service Agency. "Orders were low, and now China has stopped all agriculture purchases. I voted for Trump, but he has become the Jimmy Carter of trade!" In 1980, Jimmy Carter embargoed agricultural products to the USSR because of its invasion of Afghanistan. That action established the U.S. as an "unreliable supplier." This characterization is a real worry among U.S. small business owners.

Even though the U.S. agriculture industry did find alternative markets to sell its soybeans and other commodities to besides China from September to December 2018, it was still not enough to fill the void. A surplus was recorded, and then Mother Nature hit the Midwest farmland with historic floods that not only destroyed some crops but also delayed planting schedules because of the waterlogged fields.

The U.S. soybean trade slump continued into 2019. Brazilian soybean exports set new records as China turned to Brazil's stored soybeans instead of buying the newly harvested 2018 crop from the United States. Brazil's exports were up 85.2 percent compared to the same period in 2018. The change in trade was not a surprise to analysts who cover the sector.

Brazilian soya bean exports to China
2017 - 2019

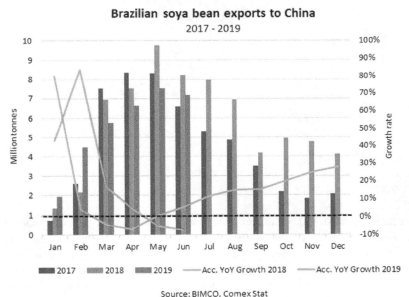

Source: BIMCO, Comex Stat

"As predicted by BIMCO earlier in the year, Brazilian soya bean exports started earlier this season, with much higher exports particularly in February," said Peter Sand, BIMCO's chief shipping analyst, in March 2019. "Brazil has managed to ramp up its exports to China in response to its increased demand for non-U.S. soya beans following the start of the trade war."

The price premiums of Brazil's soybeans have also been a good barometer on the flow of trade. When tensions increase, premiums rise. When the U.S. announced plans to go on raising the tariffs from 10 to 25 percent on $200 billion of Chinese products in May 2019, premiums increased by 7 percent. When another tariff was announced for September 1, 2019, premiums jumped 10 percent.

Brazil Soybean Premiums Are an Effective Barometer For U.S.-China Trade Tensions

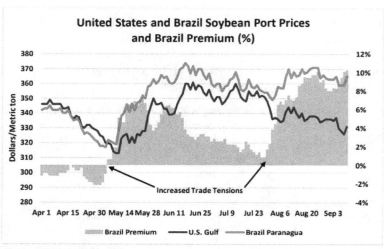

Source: USDA, September 2019

The Puzzle Pieces of Trade

The escalation of the U.S.-China trade war has had market leaders around the world voicing their concern as they look at the changing trade flow and the impact it could have on the global economy. In June 2019, the International Monetary Fund (IMF) warned in a briefing note for G-20 finance ministers and central bank governors that the U.S.-China tariffs, both those implemented and those proposed, could reduce global gross domestic product by 0.5 percent in 2020. Christine Lagarde, the IMF's managing director, said that if all the trade between the world's two largest economies were to be taxed, it would cause the $455 billion in gross domestic product to evaporate. "This amounts to a loss of about 455 billion U.S. dollars—larger than the size of the South African economy."

In my book Dynasties of the Sea: The Shipowners and Financiers Who Expanded the Era of Free Trade, Gerry Wang, Seaspan founder and former co-CEO, explained that there is a direct correlation between trade volumes and the health of a country's economy. He said that based on the lower volumes of imports into China in 2009, he and his leadership team were able to see the signs of China's slowdown six months before it was officially reported. China is the biggest consumer for many countries, and if China slows down, it needs less product. Thus the concern over global contagion.

Tariffs come at a cost
The recently announced and planned US-China tariffs could further reduce investment, productivity, and growth. Specifically, these tariffs —including those implemented last year—could reduce global GDP by 0.5 percent in 2020.

(real GDP impact of new US/China tariffs announced and envisaged in May 2019, deviations from baseline; percent difference)

(total global real GDP impact of tariffs since 2018, deviations from baseline; percent difference)

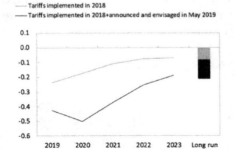

Sources: IMF, G-20 Model simulations; *World Economic Outlook*; and IMF staff calculations. Notes: The top figure shows the additional impact from the recently announced and envisaged tariffs between the US and China. The bottom figure adds the tariffs already in place since 2018. "Announced" tariffs corresponds to the increase in tariffs from 10% to 25% on $200bn of US imports as of 8 May 2019. "Envisaged" tariffs are the possible 25% tariffs on the roughly $267bn of US imports as of 13 May 2019.

INTERNATIONAL MONETARY FUND

Source: International Monetary Fund

So if a country's economy can be read in the tea leaves of tankers and container ships, can the health of trade negotiations be monitored the same way? Absolutely. In a world where political rhetoric moves the markets and makes headlines, the vessels that transport trade are the physical chess pieces being played in the trade war.

How do we read the flows? It's quite simple: When talks are going well, trade flows slightly. If talks break off, trade stops. This has been clearly documented during the current trade wars. What you need to do is shut out the noise of the daily play-by-play and look at the transactions on the water. They are monitored and announced by the U.S. ports and other government institutions like the Department of Commerce and the USTR.

The balance of trade is tracked and can be found on government websites. In black and white, the trade flows and analysis are available to anyone interested in the progress of the trade wars. All U.S. trade data is collected by the U.S. Census, which is under the jurisdiction of the U.S. Department of Commerce. There you can find all the trade data: the amount of U.S. exports that have been delivered to a country, as well as the amount of a trading partner's exports that have been received in the United States.

11

To help make sense of the data, the U.S.-China Economic and Security Review Commission (USCC) monitors and investigates the trade data and submits an annual report to Congress. The report focuses on the national security impact of the bilateral trade deal and the economic relationship between the two nations. Recommendations on all administrative or legislative actions are included in the report.

The commission's March 2019 report laid out the 2018 trade year between the two countries and offered a look at the first quarter of 2019. In the commission's own analysis, the impact of the trade war was clearly seen, based on the dramatic decrease in containers full of U.S. product being exported to China.

In 2018, U.S. goods exports dropped and the deficit was driven up to a record $419 billion—up 11.6 percent from 2017. The reason? U.S. exports to China fell by 7.4 percent to $120.3 billion, and U.S. imports from China grew by 6.7 percent to a record $539.5 billion. This has also been documented by the ports.

"China accounted for 68 percent of our container imports and 28 percent of our container exports for a total of 54 percent in 2018," explained Mario Cordero, executive director of the Port of Long Beach. "I think the main talking point here is that anytime you have a disruption at the level that we've had, it's going to be difficult for the American exporter to all of a sudden identify new markets to replace the common market they've had with Asia, more specifically China."

Figure 1: Annual Goods Trade with China, 2008—2018

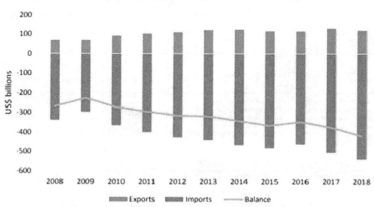

Source: U.S. Census Bureau, Trade in Goods with China, March 6, 2019. *https://www.census.gov/foreign-trade/balance/c5700.html*

According to maritime trade data, between the months of January and March 2018, U.S. gross monthly exports to China increased from $9.8 billion to $12.4

billion in anticipation of China's retaliatory tariffs. As the July date of the tariffs' implementation loomed, the number of U.S. containers and cargo increased. February monthly exports saw a 27 percent increase year-over-year.

On the other side of this trade, Chinese exports into the United States surged during April and May of 2018, from $38.2 billion in April to $43.8 billion in May, as can be seen in the chart below.

The volume of trade is an unbiased indicator of the status of trade negotiations. Both sides knew the tariffs were coming, so they needed to move their products as swiftly as possible. The commission's analysis of the full year concluded: "These trends may be due to higher import volumes ahead of the imposition of tariffs on July 6, 2018. In the second half of 2018, however, monthly U.S. exports fell precipitously, clearly visible in year-over-year change in monthly U.S. exports to China. While U.S. exports to China in July 2018 were nearly unchanged from July 2017, this was followed by a sustained decline, particularly in the last three months of 2018. Exports dropped by about 30 percent year-over-year in October, 32 percent in November, and 33 percent in December."

Figure 2: Monthly Goods Trade with China, Year-on-Year Change, January 2016 – December 2018

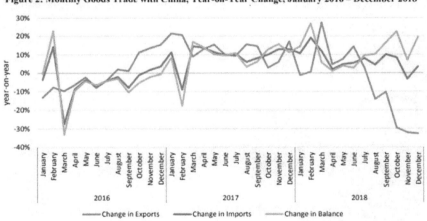

Source: U.S. Census Bureau, Trade in Goods with China, March 6, 2019. *https://www.census.gov/foreign-trade/balance/c5700.html.*

So what happened during the months leading up to the U.S. fall export drop? A number of events contributed to the contraction in trade: a ratcheting up of additional tariffs and counter tariffs between the two countries; an August meeting between then Treasury Under Secretary David Malpass and Chinese Commerce Vice Minister Wang Shouwen that ended with no resolution; and the Chinese canceling trade talks after an invitation by National Economic Adviser Larry Kudlow in September.

One result of the falling out of talks was the curtailment of U.S. agricultural products being exported to China. China had been the largest or second largest export market for U.S. agricultural products since 2010. Agricultural products were the third largest U.S. export category to China in 2017. The tariff impact was swift and hard. U.S. agricultural exports crashed from $15.9 billion in 2017 (at that time, 12 percent of all U.S. goods were exported to China) to $5.9 billion by the end of 2018 (with 4.9 percent of all U.S. goods exported to China). This was a drop of 63 percent year-over-year.

The following USDA graphics tell the story. A 2017 USDA report summarized a strong year for U.S. agricultural exports.

By the end of the 2018 trade year, China had dropped to fifth.

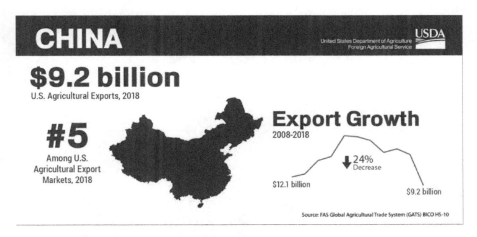

The Big Question: Who Pays the Tariffs?

The Customs Department, which is a part of Homeland Security, is the agency responsible for the administration of the customs law, which includes collecting taxes and, yes, tariffs. The subject of *who* exactly pays the tariffs has been hotly debated. President Trump has said on numerous occasions that China has "paid billions" in tariffs, and while, yes, billions have been collected, the question remains: *Who* exactly is paying?

On behalf of CNBC, in an email correspondence with U.S. Customs and Border Patrol, I asked who specifically is paying the tariffs—the countries that are exporting their product to the United States, or the U.S. importers (companies) receiving them? A CBP spokesperson responded: "The importer of record (company) is the entity that is liable and pays for the tariffs in full. That means 100 percent of all commodity lines coming into the U.S. are paid for by the U.S. importer. The importer is liable to pay that reported amount."

The CBP spokesperson explained further, "The tariff is paid either before the containers/commodities enter port, or they are paid once the shipment arrives. Payment of any duties is processed no later than 10 days later. If that amount is not payed [sic], CBP's Field Operations and eventually the Office of Finance would get involved to process any duties due."

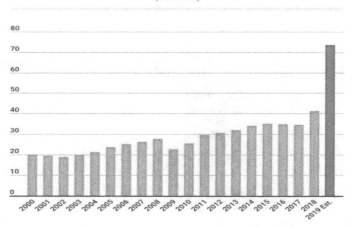

Data by fiscal year.
Sources: Office of Management and Budget (actual revenues, 2000-2018);
Congressional Budget Office (estimated revenues, 2019-2020)

FACTCHECK.ORG

Source: FactCheck.org, a project of the Annenberg Public Policy Center

This supports the complaints by the American corporations that have been voicing concern over President Trump's threat of slapping tariffs on *all* Chinese imports, saying they would need to start passing the cost on to the consumer.

"Chaos and risk will translate into a retailer's bottom line in terms of expense," explained David French, senior vice president of government relations at the National Retail Federation. "If you're trying to manage supply chain, it's the uncertainty is just adding more cost. Every time you hire a new supplier, you have to go through all sorts of supplier audits. Retailers may not want to do long-term contracts. They wanna know the capacity that manufacturer and if they can comply with U.S. consumer product safety laws, environmental regulations, and labor regulations. They don't want any surprises. So all of that takes time and energy to vet and to prove a supplier. This adds risk, which adds friction, and friction to the supply chain equals cost."

The Tale of the Tanker and Container Flow: The Truth Is There

So what does the flow of containers and tankers show? It paints two very different trade stories. When negotiations are going well, the trade of U.S. exports flows temporarily. When they break off, China doesn't buy and U.S. exports drop.

The following charts show a breakdown of the containers leaving and entering the Port of Long Beach.

This chart shows U.S. exports leaving Long Beach in 2017. Trade to China made up 39 percent.

TOP TRADING PARTNERS
CONTAINERIZED **EXPORTS**

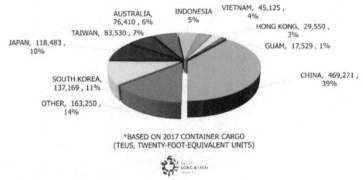

AUSTRALIA, 76,410 , 6%

INDONESIA 5%

VIETNAM, 45,125 , 4%

TAIWAN, 83,530 , 7%

HONG KONG, 29,550 , 3%

JAPAN, 118,483 , 10%

GUAM, 17,529 , 1%

SOUTH KOREA, 137,169 , 11%

CHINA, 469,271 , 39%

OTHER, 163,250 , 14%

*BASED ON 2017 CONTAINER CARGO
(TEUS, TWENTY-FOOT-EQUIVALENT UNITS)

LONG BEACH

Source: Port of Long Beach

During the trade war, U.S. exports from Long Beach to China *dropped* to 28 percent.

While U.S. exports declined, Chinese imports continued to flow in. In 2017, Chinese imports were the number one import into the Port of Long Beach, at 69 percent.

In 2018, China was still the number one import, down only by one percentage point. Nothing like U.S. exports.

TOP TRADING PARTNERS
CONTAINERIZED **EXPORTS**

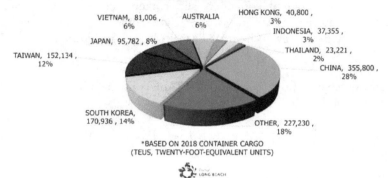

VIETNAM, 81,006, 6%

AUSTRALIA 6%

HONG KONG, 40,800, 3%

JAPAN, 95,782, 8%

INDONESIA, 37,355, 3%

TAIWAN, 152,134, 12%

THAILAND, 23,221, 2%

CHINA, 355,800, 28%

SOUTH KOREA, 170,936, 14%

OTHER, 227,230, 18%

*BASED ON 2018 CONTAINER CARGO
(TEUS, TWENTY-FOOT-EQUIVALENT UNITS)

Source: Port of Long Beach

TOP TRADING PARTNERS
CONTAINERIZED **IMPORTS**

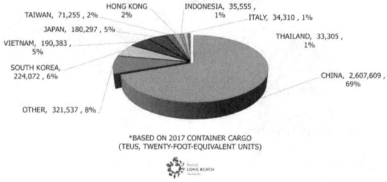

TAIWAN, 71,255, 2%

HONG KONG 2%

INDONESIA, 35,555, 1%

ITALY, 34,310, 1%

JAPAN, 180,297, 5%

VIETNAM, 190,383, 5%

THAILAND, 33,305, 1%

SOUTH KOREA, 224,072, 6%

CHINA, 2,607,609, 69%

OTHER, 321,537, 8%

*BASED ON 2017 CONTAINER CARGO
(TEUS, TWENTY-FOOT-EQUIVALENT UNITS)

Source: Port of Long Beach

"I don't think either country is winning the trade war because no one wins in a trade war," said Mario Cordero, executive director of the Port of Long Beach. "I can't say we're winning the trade war here. There has been no major concessions that the Chinese have made. We saw a noticeable drop in exports and that has continued. For example, 39 percent of our exports went to China in 2017. We haven't reached that export volume since."

TOP TRADING PARTNERS
CONTAINERIZED **IMPORTS**

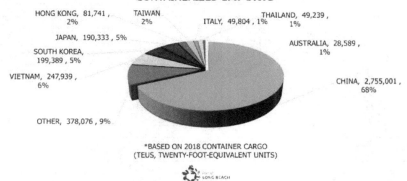

HONG KONG, 81,741, 2%

TAIWAN 2%

ITALY, 49,804, 1%

THAILAND, 49,239, 1%

JAPAN, 190,333, 5%

AUSTRALIA, 28,589, 1%

SOUTH KOREA, 199,389, 5%

VIETNAM, 247,939, 6%

CHINA, 2,755,001, 68%

OTHER, 378,076, 9%

*BASED ON 2018 CONTAINER CARGO
(TEUS, TWENTY-FOOT-EQUIVALENT UNITS)

Source: Port of Long Beach

If you think the Port of Long Beach was an anomaly in this trend, it was not. U.S. exports to China were down on a national basis. In 2018, exports were down 25 percent, and in the first quarter of 2019 they were down 33 percent.

Trade with China (Calendar Year)								
	Imports			Exports			Total	
	2017	2018	% Change	2017	2018	% Change	2017	2018	% Change
US Total	10,374,099	11,326,347	9.18%	2,781,486	2,099,275	-24.53%	13,155,585	13,425,622	2.05%
West Coast	6,640,869	7,158,921	7.80%	1,439,720	1,093,354	-24.06%	8,080,589	8,252,275	2.12%
San Pedro Bay	5,367,677	5,766,000	7.42%	979,887	764,472	-21.98%	6,347,564	6,530,472	2.88%
Los Angeles	2,759,772	3,010,804	9.10%	500,137	410,463	-17.93%	3,259,909	3,421,267	4.95%
Long Beach	2,607,905	2,755,196	5.65%	479,750	354,009	-26.21%	3,087,655	3,109,205	0.70%

Source: Port of Los Angeles, PIERS, IHS Markit

For the first half of 2019, U.S. exports on a nationwide basis were slightly up, at 1.58 percent. Capital goods like industrial machines and computers are the largest export for the United States, followed by industrial supplies; consumer goods; automotive vehicles, parts, and engines; and foods, feeds and beverages.

First Half Year US Containerized Volume (in TEU)

	2018	2019	% Change of 2018 to 2019
Exports	6,450,169	6,551,922	1.58%
Imports	11,308,277	11,666,466	3.17%
Grand Total	17,758,447	18,218,388	2.59%

Source: Port of Los Angeles, PIERS, IHS Markit

		US First Half Containerized Export Volume by Country (Jan. to Jun, in TEU)		
Rank	Country	2018	2019	% Change from 2018 to 2019
1	PEOPLES REP OF CHINA	1,194,961	927,230	-22.4%
2	JAPAN	368,536	405,854	10.1%
3	REPUBLIC OF KOREA	330,681	398,682	20.6%
4	REPUBLIC OF CHINA	299,725	327,373	9.2%
5	INDIA	285,468	293,475	2.8%
6	VIETNAM	221,106	244,072	10.4%
7	BELGIUM	194,579	212,644	9.3%
8	INDONESIA	189,191	203,178	7.4%
9	PUERTO RICO	230,979	202,580	-12.3%
10	NETHERLANDS	143,727	153,980	7.1%
11	GERMANY	132,153	140,293	6.2%
12	MALAYSIA	97,220	138,023	42.0%
13	BRAZIL	122,240	131,830	7.8%
14	THAILAND	126,950	131,812	3.8%
15	HONG KONG	110,342	126,059	14.2%
16	UNITED ARAB EMIRATES	100,226	121,470	21.2%
17	UNITED KINGDOM	112,322	118,440	5.4%
18	COLOMBIA	87,256	100,706	15.4%
19	SINGAPORE	73,758	94,758	28.5%
20	CHILE	85,584	88,408	3.3%
21	AUSTRALIA	97,739	87,464	-10.5%
22	HONDURAS	86,468	86,547	0.1%
23	GUATEMALA	82,992	82,186	-1.0%
24	DOMINICAN REPUBLIC	76,634	76,939	0.4%
25	TURKEY	81,346	75,310	-7.4%
26	SAUDI ARABIA	73,331	74,163	1.1%
27	PAKISTAN	72,575	70,945	-2.2%
28	PHILIPPINES	65,764	70,007	6.5%
29	ITALY	64,519	69,526	7.8%
30	SPAIN-S	47,460	53,068	11.8%
	Other	1,194,339	1,244,898	4.2%
	Export Total	**6,450,169**	**6,551,922**	**1.58%**

Current June export volume is tentative and has not been certified yet.

Source: OGSR

The above export breakdown shows that the United States has been successful in finding new markets for exports, albeit a small percentage. U.S. exporters are working to expand into new markets or sell more of their products to existing customers, but from a volume standpoint, even the United States' largest export destination, Japan, is half the size of China.

Trade Talk Shocks

The ebbs and flows of this trade war all hinge on promises and rhetoric. If there are signs talks are looking good, the markets pop. While that is good for investors, it doesn't measure the reality of the situation. Phrases such as "expressing optimism," "talks back on track," and "continuing negotiations" generate the biggest injections of optimism. We have also seen memorandums of understanding, but unless a transaction comes out of them, they are nothing but pieces of paper.

The biggest chess piece the Chinese have played in the trade war is the buying of soybeans. Their pledge to buy the crop and other agricultural products has been a pawn in this game, and they have moved this piece several times. China buying soybeans is deemed a win for President Trump, and it gives the impression that the Chinese are serious about negotiating. But the buy is temporary—nothing long term.

A great example of this was the temporary truce announced on December 1, 2018, between China and the United States. President Trump and China's leader Xi Jinping had a working dinner at the G-20 in Buenos Aires that ended with an agreement in which the two countries promised to refrain from increasing tariffs or imposing new tariffs for 90 days (until March 1, 2019). As part of that ceasefire, China also agreed to purchase soybeans. The details on the exact amount purchased varied depending on the news articles you read and the sources that were cited.

The U.S. Soybean Export Council cited "unidentified industry sources" who said the China Grain Reserves Corporation (Sinograin) and the country's top food company, COFCO, had purchased between and 1.5 million to 2 million metric tons of soybeans. The day after that report, the USDA disclosed sales of 1.13 million tons.

But data from BullPositions, a company that follows emerging trade trends and anomalies in the grain and oilseed markets, reported that just 545,000 tons had been shipped from Pacific ports to mainland China in the first four weeks of January 2019. During that same time frame the previous year, before the trade war had begun, 1,864,765 tons were exported to China.

Jesper Buhl, managing director of BullPositions, who analyzes the crop sales data and writes the reports, explained the reason for the varying totals: "USDA notifications on Chinese buying are confirmed commitments for Chinese buyers in a given marketing year. But Chinese buyers are free to arrange actual shipments at any time within the marketing year."

Buhl also explained there was no clarity or way to trace what was bought at what time or when these specific contracts were exported from the United States. "Weekly USDA data specification for *signed* contractual soybean sales commitments include volume and buyer nationality," he said. "The weekly data for actual *shipped* exports also includes volume and destination. There is no clear linkage between these two data specifications."

Despite the discrepancies in the sales volumes, Buhl thinks it is fair to say that China has come through on its promises when the two countries sit at the proverbial negotiation table and talk. "[The Chinese] have, since the start of the top-level trade talks in December 2018, continued to commit to buying U.S. soybeans despite the limited actual progress in the trade negotiations, and they have continued to import U.S. soybeans at a steady pace since January 2019."

So why is the *exact* container information more important for the maritime industry than the reports of a deal? Because it provides a *true* and *accurate* picture of what is going on. Maritime executives are responsible for the transportation of the trade, and they need to know the exact amounts of commodities and products purchased so they can keep track of the flow of trade. Trade is always moving—the question is: how much and where?

The rhetoric of impending trade deals being signed and the varying reports of pledges to purchase products may move the markets in drastic swings, but they don't tell the *real* story of what is going on. The only thing that matters is how much trade has been contracted and whether there are vessels that can transport it.

The data from maritime trade sources like BullPositions are used by analysts and vessel owners to help decide where they should be placing their vessels so they can compete for transport jobs. Since the trade war started, the flow of trade has changed the placement of ships. With China buying more Brazilian soybeans, the vessels that would have been coming to the United States to pick up soybeans are traveling from Brazil to China instead.

"Of the 8.2 million tons exported by Brazil in the first two months of 2019, 7 million tons have been sent to China," said Sand. "That is twice as much as was sent in the first two months of 2018 (3.5 million tons). The proportion of Brazilian soya bean exports going to China has been increasing in recent years, from 32 percent in 2005 to 82.3 percent in 2018."

Multifront Trade War

China is not the only country in the trade war arena with the United States. The United States has also launched trade wars with Canada, Mexico, the European Union, Japan, Russia, Turkey, and India. Mexico and Canada's official trade war was resolved so the three nations could move forward with U.S.–Mexico–Canada Agreement (USMCA).

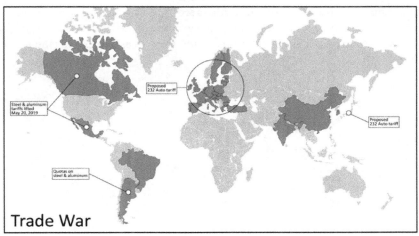

Source: Marine Money International

The E.U. has been reluctant to open its markets to U.S. agricultural competition, and the threat of auto tariffs weighs as an additional trade barrier. In addition to the trade deficit with China, the United States' trade deficit with the E.U. has ballooned to more than 11 percent in the first half of 2019.

On a global basis, the U.S. trade deficit is up 8.4 percent to $55.5 billion. The cooling off of the global economy can be seen in the global spending patterns in investment goods and consumer.

Source: Trading Economics

As we build out the pipes of trade according to the various sectors and countries targeted in this trade war, it is clear to see how the network of piping has been rerouted. The question is: Will they ever revert to their original pattern?

CHAPTER TWO

Tracking the Aluminum and Steel Trade—One Cargo at a Time

Standing by his 2016 campaign slogan "Promises Made, Promises Kept," in January 2018, President Trump made good on his pledge to U.S. steel and aluminum workers to make American steel and aluminum companies more competitive with the signing of two proclamations placing tariffs on foreign steel and aluminum imports. The tariffs were authorized on the grounds of national security, under Section 232 of the Trade Expansion Act of 1962.

Based on the flow of the cargo, in 2016, the United States was an inferior player on the world stage in both steel and aluminum production.

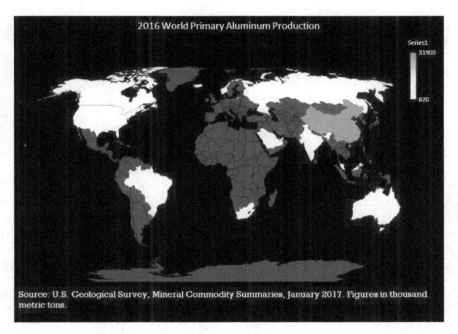

Source: U.S. Geological Survey, Mineral Commodity Summaries, January 2017. Figures in thousand metric tons.

In 2017, when President Trump officially took office, Alcoa and Century Aluminum were the only two aluminum companies operating five primary aluminum smelters in four states. Three of those smelters were operating at reduced capacity. There was also one smelter that had a status of "permanent shutdown" but was later changed to "temporary shutdown"; the owner reportedly planned to restart production in early 2018.[32] Capacity utilization of the primary smelters stood at 37 percent in 2017.[33]

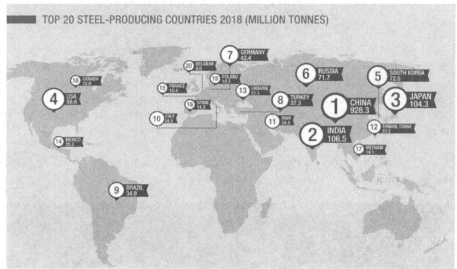

TOP 20 STEEL-PRODUCING COUNTRIES 2018 (MILLION TONNES)

Source: World Steel Association, worldsteel.org

The U.S. steel industry was comprised of seven U.S. steel producers in 2017, with a mix of foreign and domestically owned companies (Nucor, ArcelorMittal USA, and U.S. Steel) accounting for most of the U.S. steel production.[34] Capacity utilization for the U.S. steel industry was 73.9 percent that year.

China's sheer production dominance in steel and aluminum was a source of concern for U.S. companies, current and past U.S. presidents, Congress, and industry experts. The argument: China's assertive position has led to global overcapacity in both aluminum and steel, which has depressed global prices. The lower prices do not harm Chinese companies because their products are subsidized by the government to offset the price of production. The administrations of George W. Bush, Barack Obama, and Trump each met with the intergovernmental economic forum the Organisation for Economic Co-operation and Development (OECD) in multilateral discussions to address the issue.

---

[32] "Mineral Commodity Summaries 2018," U.S. Geological Survey, U.S. Department of the Interior, January 31, 2018, 20

[33] "Mineral Commodity Summaries 2018," USGS, 20

[34] International Trade Administration, Global Steel Monitor, March 2019

The Crisis in the U.S. Primary Aluminum Industry

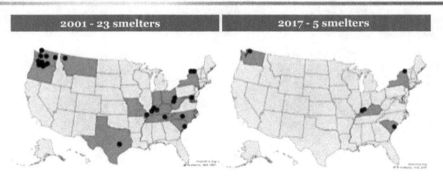

2001 - 23 smelters	2017 - 5 smelters

In 2015 alone, US producers shut or announced the closure of nearly half of the remaining US capacity.

Source: Aluminum Now

In addition to China, the volumes of cargo from South Korea, Taiwan, Italy, and India had also been identified as contributing to the global steel glut. In 2016, Lourenço Gonçalves, chairman, president, and chief executive of the mining and natural resources company Cliffs Natural Resources, told CNBC the subsidies those countries had in place created "the massive problem of dumping steel in the international market."[35]

In April 2017, President Trump took the global metals market head on and directed Commerce Secretary Ross to initiate 232 investigations into both steel and aluminum imports.

Even though the 232 guidelines gave the Department of Commerce 270 days to make its recommendations, the administration set an ambitious deadline of June 30 for the department to deliver its report.

---

[35] "China Has Conducted a 'War'—Not Trade—With Steel, Experts Say," CNBC.com, May 20, 2016, updated May 22, 2016

Share of world crude steel production 2107 & 2018

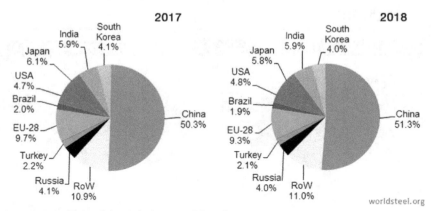

Source: World Steel Association, worldsteel.org

In a flurry of activity, the Department of Commerce called for public comments and set a hearing on steel in May and a hearing on aluminum in June.[36, 37] Hundreds of parties interested in the tariffs testified and submitted comments. Several countries came forward and asked to be removed from tariff consideration, and the European Union threatened retaliation if it was hit with tariffs.

Donald J. Trump ✔
@realDonaldTrump

I look forward to reading the @CommerceGov 232 analysis of steel and aluminum- to be released in June. Will take major action if necessary.

12:22 PM · May 27, 2017 · Twitter for iPhone

6.9K Retweets   **38.6K** Likes

During that time, hearings were conducted in which CEOs like Michael Bless of Century Aluminum and Barry Zekelman of Zekelman Industries, a consumer of steel coil, testified as to why a 232 tariff was needed for their respective

---

36   Industry and Security Bureau, "Notice Request for Public Comments and Public Hearing on Section 232 National Security Investigation of Imports of Steel," Federal Register, April 26, 2017

37   Industry and Security Bureau, "Change in Comment Deadline for Section 232 National Security Investigation of Imports of Aluminum," Federal Register, June 2, 2017

industries. Zekelman was no stranger to delivering testimony or evidence against China. In 2007, as CEO of John Maneely Company, the parent company of Wheatland Tube and Sharon Tube, he took his case against Chinese dumping steel pipe to the International Trade Commission. Wheatland Tube and Sharon Tube were two of the seven companies in the Ad Hoc Coalition.

Chinese exports of circular pipe to the United States had soared from 10,000 tons in 2002 to 750,000 tons in 2007.[38] "Our industry was socked with a 6,900 percent increase of subsidized and dumped imports!" exclaimed Zekelman. "The domestic pipe industry lost 25 percent of its total workforce when the import surge began. We also lost profitability." On June 20, 2008, the ITC ruled five to zero in the coalition's favor. Unfortunately, Zekelman soon found himself filing another case.[39]

"China started to circumvent the duties," said Zekelman. "China would either ship the product to another country or change the tariff code. By changing the country of origin or changing the tariff code on the product from standard pipe to line pipe, which doesn't have a dumping duty on it, they were able to cheat the system. China would also ship the steel at deeply discounted prices to third-party countries like South Korea, make the pipe there, and ship it in, avoiding duties. It would take us two more years to fight and win that battle. It's amazing. Just when you think you win, another battle presents itself."

Bless took the years of research and data the company had compiled on Chinese aluminum dumping and subsidies to the 232 hearings on aluminum. The company also formally filed the hundreds of pages of its presentation.

"Our research predated the 232 by several years," Bless said. "The company started its research in 2014, as things started to get ugly in the U.S. market, and then in earnest in 2015, when we were looking at the closure of all the plants and 60 percent of our military-grade plants in Hawesville. We had 400,000 pages in Mandarin that our researchers translated looking for these subsidies. We provided the Commerce Department and USTR with mountains of data that *proved* foreign producers like China were getting those subsidies. U.S. producers couldn't compete."

---

[38] "U.S. International Trade Commission (ITC) Issues Final Affirmative Vote on Antidumping and Countervailing Decisions on Circular Welded Steel Pipe From China," Business Wire, June 20, 2008

[39] "Wheatland Tube Files Duty Evasion Allegation," PR Newswire, September 15, 2016

For example, one of the biggest costs for aluminum smelters is energy.[40] "Some countries' subsidies covered that cost for them!" said Bless. "By eliminating that cost, it provided an unfair advantage where the country could overproduce product because it was so much cheaper to manufacture. In the end, companies in China are not allowed to fail, and the industry was faced with a mountain of product."

Even though China did not directly import its aluminum into the United States, by having such a dominant market share, it had the ability to impact the global price. The product was also subsidized, so it cost less for them to produce, and the depressed price did not cut into their profitability.

This was the subject of an in-depth study by the OECD that was released in January 2019. The findings of dumping and subsidies supported Century Aluminum's testimony and proved that China did indeed distort the markets with the amount of aluminum it injected into the global marketplace.

Major OECD aluminum producers are all heavily subsidized

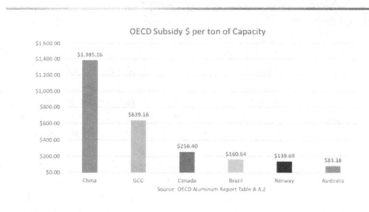

Source: Aluminum Now

---

[40] According to the Aluminum Association, electricity can account for up to 40 percent of the costs of primary unwrought aluminum production. Michael D. Platzer, "Effects of U.S. Tariff Action on U.S. Aluminum Manufacturing," Congressional Research Service, October 9, 2018

The Investigation Continued

The June deadline that President Trump had promised the nation passed with no report from the Department of Commerce. In a July 25 interview with the Wall Street Journal, President Trump explained the delay when asked why the report had not been submitted on time.

"We're waiting till we get everything completed. We don't want to do at this moment. We're going to—we're going to wait till we get everything completed here," President Trump said. "It's a very unfair situation. They're dumping steel in our country. It's extremely unfair. But we like to keep it as simple as—we like to keep complicated subjects as simple as possible. So we're waiting till we get everything finished up between health care and taxes and maybe even infrastructure. But we're going to be addressing steel dumping at a very—fairly soon."[41]

The report on the 232 on steel and aluminum was delivered to the White House on January 11, 2018. The president would have 90 days to decide on any potential action.

During the time between the initial deadline of June 30 and the actual day of the report's submission, 22,775.54 metric tons of steel were imported into the United States.[42]

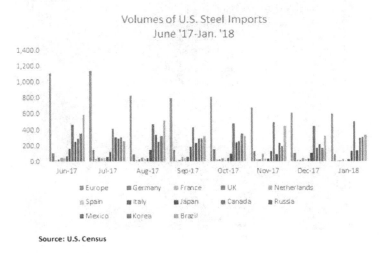

Source: U.S. Census

---

[41]   "Excerpts: Donald Trump's Interview With the Wall Street Journal," *The Wall Street Journal,* July 25, 2017

[42]   U.S. Census, 2018

Even before the 232 tariffs were initiated, the U.S.-based trading house now known as Castleton Commodities International was making large strategic buys of aluminum, stockpiling hundreds of thousands of tons of aluminum near a bend in the Mississippi River outside New Orleans. The trader started the purchases in 2016, ahead of the sanctions against Russia's aluminum company United Co. Rusal and President Trump's aluminum tariffs. In April 2018, news reports said the amount was so large you could see the stockpile from space. The proof was in the Google Maps images. "It was a proverbial gold mine of inventory," remarked Anton Posner, CEO of the global logistics company Mercury Resources.

Source: Google Earth

During the company's early spring board of directors meeting, Bless presented the restart plan and recommended the board review and approve it so that if President Trump did move forward with the 232 they would be ready to restart operations. The contingency plan recommended the company take two immediate actions: restart its Hawesville facility, and invest in their other plants. "The investment to get the Hawesville plant producing again was $150 million, not only to rebuild the pot lines that had been shut but to rebuild the other two lines that we hadn't rebuilt in way too long. They were way past their economic lives," Bless said. "We told our directors, on a like-for-like basis, we ought to invest more money and make this plant productive and efficient, because we think this is gonna be a globally competitive plant, based on U.S. power prices and U.S. technical advancements."

Bless said he advised the board to look at their other plants through the same investment lens. "Those investments were smaller because they hadn't been shut to the extent Hawesville was, but we also put in place plans to increase their value as well. It was needed if the 232 was lifted. Our board provisionally approved the plans." Now Century Aluminum and the world waited for President Trump to make his decision.

Donald J. Trump @
@realDonaldTrump

Our Steel and Aluminum industries (and many others) have been decimated by decades of unfair trade and bad policy with countries from around the world. We must not let our country, companies and workers be taken advantage of any longer. We want free, fair and SMART TRADE!

7:12 AM · Mar 1, 2018 · Twitter for iPhone

20.1K Retweets   **95.6K** Likes

In late February 2018, Bless received an invitation to attend a meeting with President Trump along with other steel and aluminum CEOs and industry leaders on March 1. The president took to Twitter ahead of the meeting.

"Never in my career had I spent a lot of time with politicians, and certainly not with the president of the United States," said Bless. "I found the whole meeting fascinating. If you forgot about where you were for a second, it was just like any standard business meeting conducted by a CEO. But in this meeting, the CEO figure happened to be the president! At the end of the meeting, he announced his decision to move forward to the 232. It was a surprise to us all that he was gonna to announce his decision at that meeting." The tariffs would be at 25 percent on steel imports and 10 percent on aluminum imports from all originating countries with the exception of Australia, Brazil, and Argentina.

That afternoon, Zekelman sent a letter out to his North American employees announcing that everyone would receive a $1,000 annual bonus once the tariffs went into effect and would be paid that bonus annually for as long the tariffs remained in place. In the letter, Zekelman wrote: "Together, we have sacrificed and worked hard to become the best pipe and tube manufacturer in the world. The policies announced today will have a tremendous positive impact on our ability to compete and thrive. The playing field is being leveled and WE WILL WIN IN A FAIR FIGHT."[43]

The Rush to Beat the Tariff

When the news was announced, Anton Posner's phone lit up with concerned clients. "We saw our trader clients working to rush in aluminum and steel before the tariffs were imposed," Posner said. "There was not a lot of time. Everything went into motion on changing U.S. ports in an effort to get the cargo in before the tariffs went into effect."

Clients asked Posner to run various cost basis scenarios. One was diverting aluminum orders bound for the United States to Mexico instead. "As soon as the news broke about the tariffs, the response from clients was pretty quick," he said. "Most of our clients are traders, so they are somewhat reactionary, versus producers and consumers, who are more thoughtful and plan ahead."

The aluminum traders Posner services buy primary aluminum that is then sold to aluminum rolling companies like Arconic. Posner recalled one rebar shipment that was caught up in the tariff countdown. "This shipment was scheduled to load in two weeks and then head over to the United States for a two-week voyage to the Gulf of Mexico. As soon as the tariff was announced, we had an automatic limitation in getting the commodities in. Based on the time of loading and travel, it would never make it to the U.S. in time before the tariffs were imposed. We immediately called one of our clients who was a trader who had that impending order and asked them what they wanted to do. They were so surprised; they didn't know immediately. They told me they had to call the steel mill in Turkey."

A few days later Posner received the trader's call.

"They wanted to cancel the ship because there was no way to load the cargo and bring it to the States in time before the tariff. So I would have to renegotiate a way out of the freight and pay a hundred grand for wasting the

---

[43]   Zekelman letter to employees, March 1, 2018

shipowner's time. I would rather do that than take a multimillion dollar hit on a ship loaded with Turkish rebar with no place to go," Posner said. "The trader then went to Italy, literally *and* figuratively, and worked with the Italian rebar mill to replace the supply they canceled. The company had never exported to the States before, so the trader had to go and do a lot of hand-holding and teach them how to prep and load the vessel properly. It was a lot of work to get it done right, but in the end the trader would rather pay and absorb the 25 percent tariff on Italian steel than the 50 percent tariff on Turkish steel."[44]

Donald J. Trump ✅
@realDonaldTrump

I have just authorized a doubling of Tariffs on Steel and Aluminum with respect to Turkey as their currency, the Turkish Lira, slides rapidly downward against our very strong Dollar! Aluminum will now be 20% and Steel 50%. Our relations with Turkey are not good at this time!

8:47 AM · Aug 10, 2018 · Twitter for iPhone

John Foster, president of Kurt Orban Partners, which specializes in the trading of steel, said ships carrying steel cargo were also in a race to beat the clock. "You had ships trying to offload cargo at earlier ports of discharge in order to get in prior to tariffs starting," he said. "For example, a Turkish vessel, instead of traveling to the Gulf to discharge, came into a port in the Northeast because if they traveled to the Gulf their product might not have made it through customs in time prior to the tariff implementation."

Once the tariffs were imposed, Posner said, the flow of trade changed immediately. "We started to see aluminum coming in from Alcoa in Australia and other non-tariffed producers. Australia was exempted from the tariffs. So containers started to flow into the West Coast and U.S. Gulf," Posner explained. "Australian aluminum, typically, was fed into the Asian markets because it was closer in distance. The only way a company like Alcoa would decide to take on the longer freight distance was because it would have significant tariff advantage. In the end, they did decide to go the longer freight route to capitalize on the tariff situation, so that move hurt smaller aluminum players in South Africa who serviced the United States."

Trade by sea wasn't the only part of the trade plumbing that changed. "Canada, which was the largest supplier of steel to the United States, diverted its rail freight from the Quebec smelters traditionally bound for the United States and found customers in Europe," Posner explained. "That spigot got immediately

---

[44] On August 13, 2018, President Trump raised Turkey's tariff from 25 percent to 50 percent. President Trump later lowered the tariff on Turkish steel from 50 percent to 25 percent.

turned off—and by 'immediately,' I mean within a month or so. That route of trade moved from land to the ocean."

The Tariffs Begin

On March 8, 2019, President Trump signed the 232 proclamations, imposing a 10 percent tariff on aluminum imports and a 25 percent tariff on steel imports. In the room to witness the ceremony was a group of aluminum and steel workers from U.S. companies. Century Aluminum sent three production workers from the Hawesville military-grade plant to be present for the signing. "The whole process was surreal. Sonia, James, and Dusty were there, standing behind the president when he was at the podium," Bless said. "I watched it on TV from our plant in Hawesville with our employees there. The whole experience was quite amazing."

The crunch was on the U.S. companies to turn up domestic production. While the companies were in the process of increasing capacity, that didn't mean imports were not being purchased. Even at top capacity, U.S. steel and aluminum companies could not meet domestic demand.

"It took a couple of months for us to get out of the starter's block," said Bless, "because the first thing you have to start doing is hiring folks. We did not want to hire people on the hopes the 232 would be signed. The last thing we would ever want to do is hire somebody and then lay them off. That would have been a disaster."

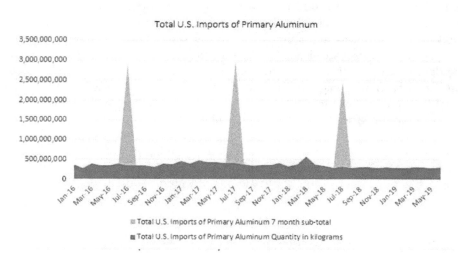

Source: American Primary Aluminum Association (APAA)

36

Bless said it took about two months to find the skilled labor they needed. In the meantime, Century Aluminum started going down its reinvestment checklist to get ready to increase production. Both industries buoyed when the tariffs initially took effect. The impact of both tariffs can be seen in the decreasing volume of cargo ships carrying steel and aluminum into the United States.

Primary Aluminum								
	2012	2013	2014	2015	2016	2017	2018	2019
U.S. Production (1,000 metric tons)	2,070	1,948	1,718	1,589	826	744	905	1,268
Total U.S. imports (1,000 metric tons)	2,927	3,162	3,327	3,397	4,267	4,877	4,179	
Imports from Canada (1,000 metric tons)	1,918	2,274	2,215	2,236	2,307	2,460	2,151	
Imports from GCC (1,000 metric tons)	413	375	421	530	840	934	916	
Imports from India (1,000 metric tons)	2	0	0	39	27	121	181	
All other imports (1,000 metric tons)	594	513	690	592	1,094	1,362	931	

Source: CRU and USITC Dataweb.

The decrease in the amount of foreign aluminum gave U.S. aluminum makers the ability to increase production.

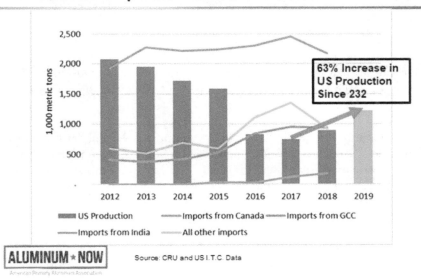

Source: Aluminum Now

Tale of the Steel Tariff

When the steel tariff when into effect, U.S. steel imports went down. According to the U.S. Census Bureau, in 2018 the average monthly volume of steel imports was down 26.2 percent from the 2017 monthly volume of 2.5 million metric tons. The decrease continued into 2019. From January to May 2019, the United States imported 12.3 million metric tons of steel. That was an 11.6 percent decrease from the 13.9 million metric tons imported in 2018 over the same period. From a value designation, imports decreased to $11.3 billion—a 15 percent decrease from the $13.3 billion in 2018.[45]

**U.S. Imports of All Steel Mill Products
From World**

SOURCE: U.S. Department of Commerce, Enforcement and Compliance
Graph last modified on: July 24, 2019 with
Licensing Data collected through July 24, 2019
Commerce license data used for the last months appear in a different color
Data extracted from the import licenses are not official Census data

The countries that imported the most steel to the United States in the first five months of 2019 were Brazil, at 19.7 percent; followed by Canada, at 14.9 percent; and Mexico, at 10.4 percent.[46]

During this time frame, the United States imported 4.0 million metric tons of flat products, accounting for 32.8 percent of total steel mill imports. Meanwhile, 3.3 million metric tons of semi-finished products were imported, contributing to 26.7 percent of total imports.

---

[45] "Steel Industry Executive Summary," International Trade Administration, U.S. Department of Commerce, July 2019

[46] "Steel Industry Executive Summary," U.S. Department of Commerce, July 2019

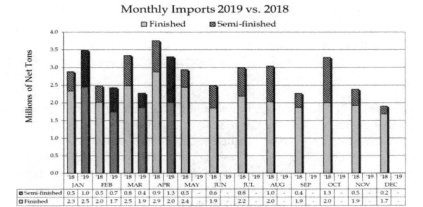

Monthly Imports 2019 vs. 2018

□ Finished ▨ Semi-finished

	'18 '19 JAN	'18 '19 FEB	'18 '19 MAR	'18 '19 APR	'18 '19 MAY	'18 '19 JUN	'18 '19 JUL	'18 '19 AUG	'18 '19 SEP	'18 '19 OCT	'18 '19 NOV	'18 '19 DEC
▨ Semi-finished	0.5 1.0	0.5 0.7	0.8 0.4	0.9 1.3	0.5 -	0.6 -	0.8 -	1.0 -	0.4 -	1.3 -	0.5 -	0.2 -
□ Finished	2.3 2.5	2.0 1.7	2.5 1.9	2.9 2.0	2.4 -	1.9 -	2.2 -	2.0 -	1.9 -	2.0 -	1.9 -	1.7 -

% change finished imports April 2019 vs.April 2018 -30.1%

Source: American Iron and Steel Institute

U.S. steel production up was up 3.1 percent.

U.S. steel exports had been relatively flat from 2009 to 2018.[47] After the tariff was imposed, the flow of trade for the U.S. steel industry changed in a positive direction. The tariffs were doing their job.

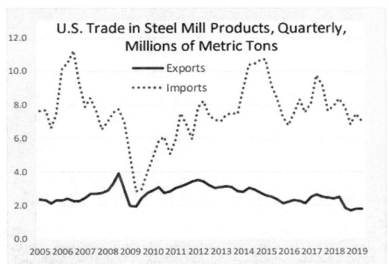

U.S. Trade in Steel Mill Products, Quarterly, Millions of Metric Tons

—— Exports
······ Imports

Source: U.S. Department of Commerce, IHS Markit Global Trade Atlas, World Steel Report: September 2019

Source: World Steel Association, worldsteel.org

---

[47] "Steel Industry Executive Summary," U.S. Department of Commerce, July 2019

Because of the decrease in steel imports and the increase in U.S. steel exports, the trade gap narrowed by 30.3 percent in 2019 compared to one year ago. Breaking it down by the cargo: the volume of U.S. steel exports increased by 4.6 percent from April 2019 to May 2019. Steel imports during the same time frame decreased by 37.8 percent.[48]

Statistics from the Bureau of Labor show that the number of people working in iron and steel mills increased from 82,087 when the 232 tariffs were levied to 84,913 in December of 2018. United States Steel Corporation also reopened two blast furnaces. Things were looking good. On the pricing side, the tariffs gave the U.S. companies the ability to raise prices to just under the tariff prices of their competitors so they could make a profit and still be the less expensive alternative. But the positives were short-lived.

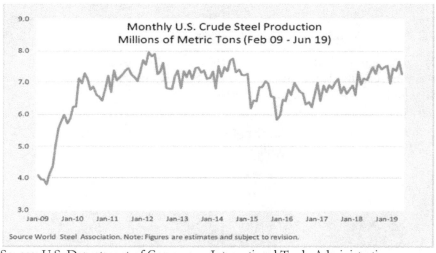

Source: U.S. Department of Commerce, International Trade Administration

"The 232 was like a supercharge to the industry, and it made steel and aluminum companies a lot of money over a short period of time," explained David Lipschitz, senior analyst of metals, mining, steel and coal commodities and global markets at Macquarie Capital Inc. "The problem was that at the end of the day the tariffs stimulated more production, and that extra capacity eventually depressed steel prices. The natural progression of supply and demand was thrown out of whack."

---

[48] "Steel Industry Executive Summary," U.S. Department of Commerce, July 2019

After the price peak in the third quarter of 2018, the benchmark for domestic steel prices started descending in the fourth quarter. Companies that produce commodities depend on a strong price for profitability.

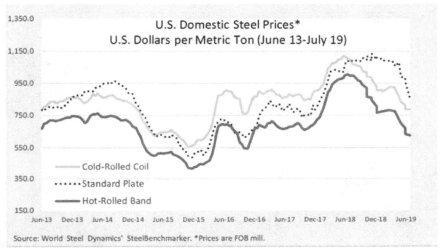

Source: U.S. Department of Commerce, International Trade Administration

The overcapacity of steel in the market was dubbed "Steelmageddon."[49]

Since 2017, steel production has steadily increased. In 2017, production grew from 81.6 million metrics tons (MMT) in 2017 to 86.6 MMT in 2018.[50] According to the September 2019 Steel Imports Report by the International Trade Administration, production further increased 5.2 percent from 42.1 MMT in YTD 2018 to 44.3 MMT in YTD 2019.[51]

Comparing production to consumption, which is a measure of steel demand, consumption has exceeded U.S. production since 2009. The gap between the two has decreased in the first seven months of 2019. After the 232, the imports have also steadily decreased.

In June 2019, U.S. Steel announced it would be temporarily idling two blast furnaces in the United States (its Gary Works plant in Indiana and B2 blast furnace at Great Lake Works), as well as a blast furnace in Europe. The

---

[49]   Timna Taners, August 2019
[50]   ITA Global Steel Monitor, U.S., September 2019
[51]   ITA Global Steel Monitor, U.S., September 2019

company also announced it was scaling back its projected steel shipments for 2019 but was still anticipating a 5 percent increase from the previous year.

Steel Imports Report: **United States**

Overall Production and Import Penetration

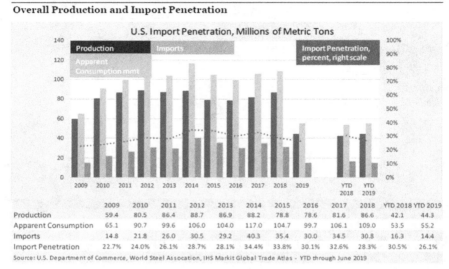

	2009	2010	2011	2012	2013	2014	2015	2016	2017	2018	YTD 2018	YTD 2019
Production	59.4	80.5	86.4	88.7	86.9	88.2	78.8	78.6	81.6	86.6	42.1	44.3
Apparent Consumption	65.1	90.7	99.6	106.0	104.0	117.0	104.7	99.7	106.1	109.0	53.5	55.2
Imports	14.8	21.8	26.0	30.5	29.2	40.3	35.4	30.0	34.5	30.8	16.3	14.4
Import Penetration	22.7%	24.0%	26.1%	28.7%	28.1%	34.4%	33.8%	30.1%	32.6%	28.3%	30.5%	26.1%

Source: U.S. Department of Commerce, World Steel Assocation, IHS Markit Global Trade Atlas - YTD through June 2019

"As we indicated in communications issued June 18, we have made operational adjustments to our global blast furnace footprint to align with current market conditions," U.S. Steel spokesperson Meghan Cox said. "As a result, we have issued [WARN] notices in the event of possible future layoffs as a result of our reduced production levels at Great Lakes Works. We are taking this step to inform employees and relevant stakeholders of possible future impacts."[52]

U.S. Steel wasn't the only company in the sector to be impacted by the headwinds of lower steel prices and the steel glut. In the second quarter of 2019, the average share prices for all the charted steel stocks decreased from the first quarter of 2019 average.[53]

U.S. Steel saw the largest decrease in average share price, dropping from the previous quarter by 27.2 percent. AK Steel saw a decrease of 17.3 percent;

---

[52] Joseph S. Pete, "U.S. Steel May Lay Off 200 in Michigan as It Idles Blast Furnaces in Gary and at Great Lakes Works," Indiana Economic Digest, August 20, 2019

[53] U.S. Department of Commerce, International Trade Administration, Global Steel Trade Monitor, Steel Imports Report: United States, September 2019

ArcelorMittal, 14.7 percent; Steel Dynamics, 13.6 percent; and Nucor, 6.1 percent.

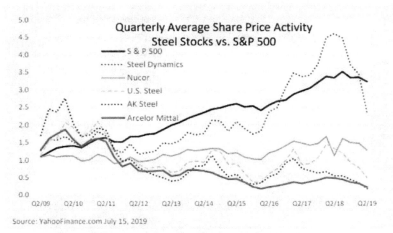

Source: Department of Commerce, International Trade Administration

"What's happening is we're finding that healthy balancing point in pricing," said Zekelman. "Only 20 million tons of steel imports are needed to support our market. We know we can add capacity, because the U.S. steel market produces about 95 to 100 million tons and could displace the imports with added efficient capacity. You'll also find a balance point in operating rates. In the end, the market will take care of itself and the people will reinvest."

Zekelman said he had to pass the cost of the increase in price on to his customers. It was unavoidable. "The price of steel should stabilize as long as these things are kept in place. We can have a healthy domestic steel industry."

While U.S. steel companies had to pull back production, China did the exact opposite, continuing to produce record amounts of steel to remain the number one producer of steel in the world.

China produced 87.53 million tons of crude steel in June 2019, down from the record 89.09 million tons in May.[54] The reason for the slight drop was the government's effort to cut smog in the northern province of Hebei, which is

---

[54]   Muyu Xu, Tom Daly, "China Churns Out Record Daily Steel Output in June," Reuters, July 14, 2019

the country's biggest steel producing territory. The drop however was still above the 80.2 million tons in June 2018.[55]

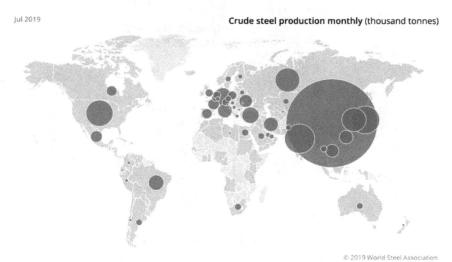

Source: World Steel Association, worldsteel.org

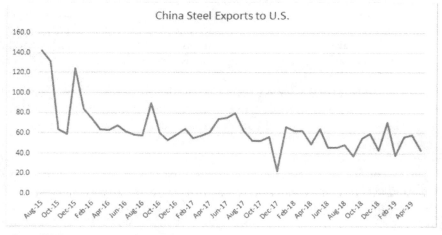

Source: U.S. Census

---

[55]   Muyu Xu, Tom Daly, "China Churns Out Record Daily Steel Output in June," Reuters, July 14, 2019

On July 15, 2019, President Trump tripled down on his plan to increase demand for domestic steel with his executive order "Buy American III," which mandated the greater use of U.S. steel and iron in federal infrastructure projects. The order would gradually increase the minimum amount of U.S. steel and iron products required to be used in federal projects from 50 percent to 75 percent to 95 percent.

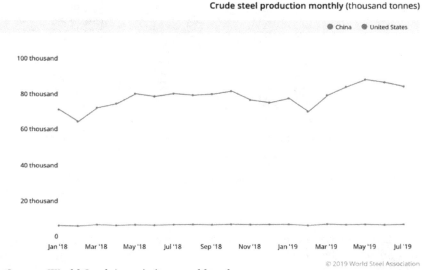

Crude steel production monthly (thousand tonnes)

● China ● United States

© 2019 World Steel Association

Source: World Steel Association, worldsteel.org

Aluminum's 232 Journey

Prior to the implementation of the 232 tariffs, the U.S. aluminum industry was producing around 13 percent of total U.S. consumption. Domestic secondary production of old scrap was at 27 percent, and imports were 60 percent.[56] Fast forward to 2019, and the story of aluminum has changed.

"The tariffs have worked exactly as they were intended to," said Bless. "As long as the subsidies are offset by the 232 tariffs, we could sell everything we make in the U.S. 10 times over. You saw U.S. production—not only our plant, but others—proceed to restart immediately. In fact, U.S. production will be 60 percent higher by the end of 2019 than it was before the president ordered the remedy."

---

[56] "Effects of U.S. Tariff Action on U.S. Aluminum Manufacturing," Congressional Research Service, October 9, 2018

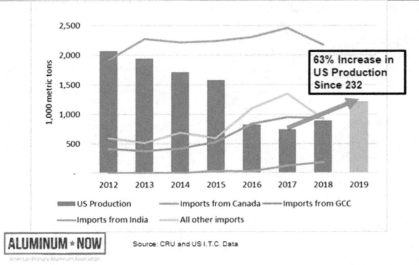

Aluminum 232 Having Desired Effect: Domestic Production Up 63% from 2017 Levels

Source: Aluminum Now

The 232 tariffs gave the aluminum industry what it needed to reinvest and grow. But unfortunately, they also fueled many different trade wars and led to retaliatory tariffs being levied against the United States.

"The 232 impact on steel and aluminum was very similar to the tariffs on washing machines," explained Erin Ennis, former senior vice president of the U.S.-China Business Council, which represents 200 U.S. companies that do business with China. "While it had a nominal effect on Chinese imports, it burned a bridge for the United States with our other trading partners. The tariff essentially created a multifront battle with the countries that are actually more likely to be our ally in going after some of China's trading practices. Now they are part of the war." Countries imposing tariffs on U.S. products as retaliation for the 232 tariffs on steel and aluminum initially included Mexico, Canada, India, Japan, Russia, and Turkey, as well as the European Union.

The retaliatory tariffs were not the only negative influences on the steel and aluminum sectors. The rhetoric of the trade war had an impact as well. For example, aluminum prices tumbled to their lowest level in several weeks at the start of August 2019 after President Trump shocked the global markets by announcing that the United States would add a 10 percent tariff on the remaining $300 billion of Chinese imports, starting September 1. Twelve days later, the USTR announced it had revised the list of tariffs to be implemented in September to exclude certain products including cell phones, laptops, and video game consoles until December 15. The markets surged. President Trump told the galley of reporters that he was delaying the tariffs after a "very good call" with the Chinese, adding, "We're doing this for Christmas season, just in case some of the tariffs would have an impact on U.S. customers."[57]

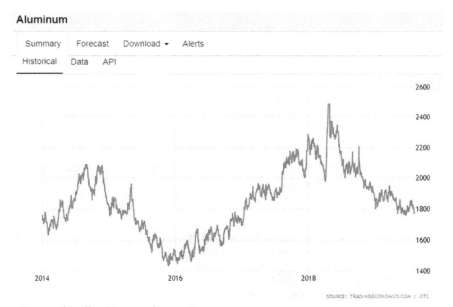

Source: Trading Economics

In addition to the status of trade talks, Bless explained, global monetary policy was a factor that could influence domestic demand and production for the second half of 2019. The flow of trade has shown the slowing of the global economy. The trade data has sparked concern with central banks around the world, triggering a race to the bottom of low interest rates to stave off a downturn. This environment stoked President Trump in his urging the Federal Reserve to competitively cut rates.

After the July 2019 rate cut, President Trump's displeasure toward the Federal Reserve increased. President Trump criticized the Fed for not lowering rates to the level he would like.

---

[57]   President Donald Trump to Reporter Galley, August 13, 2019

He has even suggested that the Fed is the real problem with the U.S. economy.

One of the key reasons why President Trump wants monetary easing and Bless mentioned monetary policy as a possible market influencer for aluminum is the historical *inverse* relationship between commodity prices and interest rates. The connection? Raw material prices and interest rates are closely correlated to the cost of the commodity. When interest rates move lower, commodities normally rise in price. Commodity producers like Century Aluminum make money when prices are higher. For an added bonus, if you are a retailer, manufacturer, or producer, the cost associated with storing that commodity is cheaper in a low-interest rate environment—not to mention that borrowing money at a lower rate is a positive as well. The lower borrowing rates provide a sugar high for the markets.

This chart shows the pattern.

Percentage Gain/Loss in S&P 500				
Rate cuts	Day of	One month later	3 months later	6 months later
25-basis-point cut	0.16%	0.57%	3.67%	5.64%
50-basis-point cut	0.34%	1.25%	-1.36%	-3.58%
75-basis-point cut	2.76%	0.27%	-3.97%	-4.01%

Graph: Marine Money International

Since 1990, every time there has been a 25-basis-point cut, the S&P 500 has gained on average 0.16 percent that day. If the cut is doubled, the market is 0.34 percent higher on the day of the decision and 1.25 percent higher one month later. The most powerful cut, according to market history, has been the 75-basis-point reduction, which has stimulated a 2.76 percent rally on average—but only a 0.27 percent gain 30 days later.

In addition to rate cuts, President Trump has also started using Twitter as a platform to make his case for a lower dollar. This too would help manufacturers and producers: Their exports could gain market share because they are less expensive compared to exports from countries with stronger currencies. That could help increase U.S. exports that have declined.

The other reason for a lower dollar is to make the United States an attractive place to set up shop instead of manufacturing overseas. These two economic policies that President Trump is advocating for would benefit the industries he has been trying to make "competitive" and encourage companies to avoid tariffs by making their products in America. The flow of the containers and cargo would also shift if it happened.

The global slowdown has also played a role in commodity production. This makes sense because if there is no growth, there will be less demand. Also, if there is less growth, that would translate into less revenue, which means less spending. According to the International Aluminum Institute (IAI), global aluminum production fell by 0.5 percent in the first half of 2019. That would be the first year-over-year decline since the Global Financial Crisis of 2009. Chinese aluminum output dropped 3.1 percent from June 2018 to June 2019. However, that global decrease in production did not impact China's standing as the number one aluminum producer in the world.

With the decrease in global production, aluminum stocks (inventories) around the world continued to fall, both in warehouses and other areas of storage. "They currently sit at levels generally considered to indicate real tightness in supply," remarked Bless. "The balanced forecast is underpinned by only modest consumption growth expectations. With the outlook on China growing less than 2 percent for the full year and the world essentially flat, we are looking at a basically flat 2019 versus 2018."

Total for Jun 2014 to Jun 2019: 310,144 thousand metric tonnes of aluminium

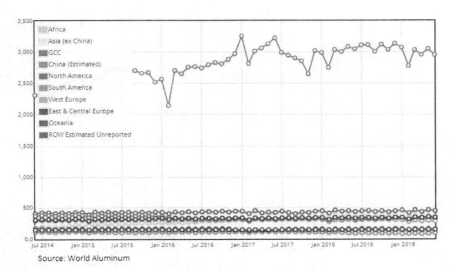

Source: World Aluminum

Despite the progress the U.S. aluminum industry has seen because of the 232 tariffs, Bless stressed that the aluminum industry is still recovering. "Even with the U.S. available production coming back on fully, at 60 percent the U.S. still needs to import a lot of aluminum," he said. "Unfortunately, when the president ordered the remedy, we had millions and millions of tons of production shut down. The U.S. used to be able to produce the majority of its aluminum needs. Going back to 2015, before President Trump, it was between 10 and 13 percent. Today we're probably close to 20 percent. That's a 60 percent increase in production coming back on."

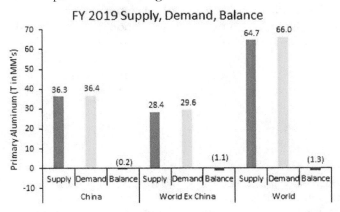

Source: Century Aluminum

Changes in the Flow of Steel and Aluminum Trade

On May 17, 2019, more than a year after the 232 tariffs were imposed, the USTR announced an agreement with Canada and Mexico that would remove the two nations from the steel and aluminum tariff list. In exchange, Canada and Mexico would remove all retaliatory tariffs on American products. Aggressive monitoring and a mechanism to prevent surges of steel and aluminum imports from both countries would be put in place. "We are watching this very closely," said Bless. "Just as long as the monitoring and enforcement that the USTR talked about is followed through by Congress, we are not concerned. If the USTR sees a surge, the tariff goes back on. We think everybody understands the agreement."

Zekelman echoed Bless sentiments. "The administration used the 232 successfully to speed up the USMCA [United States–Mexico–Canada Agreement] negotiations, which were dragging on far too long. We believe that Canada and Mexico will have to address transshipment of foreign steel through their countries that is headed to the U.S. to avoid the return of the 232 duties.[58] The U.S. is closely monitoring any surge in steel products and will promptly address any surge with duties or even quotas. Ultimately we are pleased."

Guillermo Malpica, former trade negotiator and former Head of the Mexican Trade and NAFTA Office in Washington, D.C. explained the timing of the negotiations. "While for political reasons it was unviable to discuss and ratify the USMCA with the tariffs on steel and aluminum still pending to solution," he said. "The fact of solving that irritant was not a factor in the decision of the Mexican Senate to assess and ratify the new NAFTA."

In the end, despite the headwinds of the retaliatory tariffs and slowing domestic and global economies, based on the consumption of aluminum, Bless said he is optimistic. "We see record order rates because the U.S. is so terribly under-supplied, but the ultimate health of the market is critical to our future production. At the end of the day, low prices really don't matter as much. You can't sell your product if customers don't want it."

---

[58] Transshipment is the shipment of goods to an intermediate destination before arriving at its final destination. In shipping that can change the "origin" of the product from the original location to the intermediate location. This method has been used to avoid paying tariffs.

CHAPTER THREE

U.S. Agriculture Sales Spoil

After the 232 tariffs on steel and aluminum were imposed, China struck back, slapping retaliatory tariffs on almost all U.S. food and agriculture exports. Soybeans, the second most planted field crop in the United States, quickly became the poster child of pain for the trade war. The politically calculated retaliatory tariffs by the Chinese focused on the farming belt—one of the voter bases that helped Trump win the 2016 election. It was a calculated move. In 2017, U.S. agriculture products to China topped around $16 billion. China isn't the only country hitting the agriculture industry. The European Union and India have also levied retaliatory tariffs.

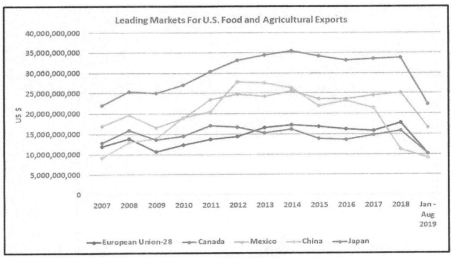

Source: USDA Global Access Trading System (GATS). Values are not adjusted for inflation

The major pipes of soybean trade run between the United States, the world's largest soybean producer; China, the largest consumer and importer of uncrushed soybeans; and Brazil, the largest exporter of soybeans.

Just weeks after the April 4 announcement of China's retaliatory tariffs, trade negotiators from the United States and China met in Beijing, but no resolution was made. The world had a front-row seat to the reality trade show.

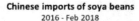

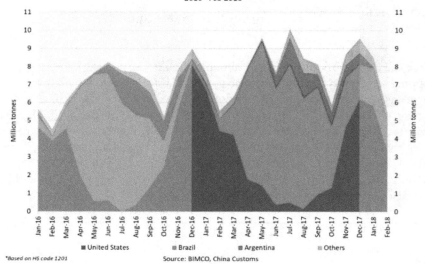

According to USDA data on U.S. soybean sales, the last meaningful buy of soybeans before the intermittent buying began was made on April 12, 2018.

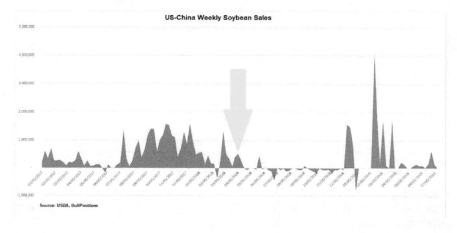

After that, the slide of soybean sales began. "Purchase prices can be made, but sales can always be canceled, so nothing is final until it is in country," explained Michael Nepveux, economist for the Farm Bureau.

In May, just two months before the trade war officially began, a plot twist occurred. China's second largest telecommmunications company, ZTE, was brought into the trade discussions by China. Reports said the Chinese would remove tariffs on certain agricultural products in exchange for a reprieve from the crippling U.S. sanctions on ZTE. In a tweet, President Trump promised to help ZTE, setting off bipartisan uproar. Days later, China's Commerce Ministry announced it would stop tariffs on U.S. sorghum in trade talks. The trade war was on hold, and China reportedly agreed to purchase more U.S. goods. President Trump announced the news on Twitter.

The news ignited soybean futures and hopes in the agriculture industry. But the goodwill gesture by the Chinese, promising "massive" amounts of purchases, did not materialize. "I think the problem is we don't actually get a good understanding of what is actually agreed to in the various meetings," said Jim Sutter, CEO of the U.S. Soybean Export.

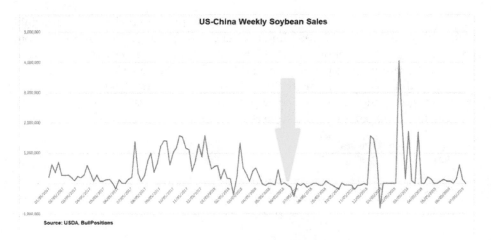

US-China Weekly Soybean Sales

Source: USDA, BullPositions

Figure 1. Soybean Exports to China by Port for 2017/18 and 2018/19
First Seven Weeks of the Marketing Year

2017/18
27 mbu

PUGET
SOUND

2018/19
2.5 mbu

INTERIOR
2017/18
2.7 mbu

2017/18
51 mbu

COLUMBIA
RIVER

2018/19
2.5 mbu

2017/18
150 mbu

MISSISSIPPI RIVER

SOUTH ATLANTIC
2017/18
3.8 mbu

EAST GULF
2017/18
3.7 mbu

FARM BUREAU
Source: USDA Federal Grain Inspection Service, Farm Bureau Calculations

2018/19
2.4 mbu

On June 15, the United States set July 6 as the effective date for the 25 percent tariff on $34 billion of Chinese imports. An additional 25 percent tariff would also kick in on an another $16 billion of imports after a public comment period. China shot back with tariffs on $34 billion of U.S. products. Farmers were faced with an unprecedented unknown. On July 6, agriculture purchases by China dried up. Sales of soybeans died on the vine. Shipments fell by 98 percent along the Mississippi River, 95 percent along the Columbia River, and 91 percent from Puget Sound. No massive amount of shipments out of the eastern Gulf regions, the South Atlantic, or the interior were made.

"Ninety-five percent of the people on the planet live outside of the U.S., so trade is our business plan, it's our marketing plan," explained Gibbs. "Those countries involved in the 232 retaliated, and essentially, in China's case, they took our products off the market immediately with retaliatory tariffs. We lost a third of our market literally overnight. It was a market that we built ourselves over 30 years. We built that Asian market!"

The Soybean Season

Unlike commodities and products that can be produced at any time, agriculture products have a specific schedule. They are also not typically influenced by geopolitical events. "Some think a farmer can just throw in a new crop to grow if one crop falls out of favor," explained Gibbs. "You can't do that. The machinery on a farm is crop specific. It's not one-size-fits-all. You also have certain trailers that move specific crops. There are a lot of factors that play into a farmer's crop plan."

For soybean farmers like Gibbs, the business of the bean starts two weeks after the last frost in spring. That's when the soybean seeds are planted. The United States' soybean crop is mostly grown in the Midwest and Delta regions. The soybeans begin to mature in late August in the South, and September in the Midwest. By October, the soybeans are ready to be harvested and become available to potential buyers. This is a critical time for the industry, as the full U.S. supply begins to become known.

The marketing year for that harvest starts on September 1, while the crops are maturing, and runs through August of the following year. Once harvested, the beans are either readied for export or stored in grain elevators. Orders are placed as early as August or September, once the buyers get a sense of the crop. Because of the way the marketing extends over two years, that crop is identified over a two-year span. For example, the 2018 crop would be identified as the 2018/2019 crop.

"We tend to ship the bulk of our soybeans exports to China right after harvest in the fall, which in 2018 was prime trade war time, so we missed out on that last year," said Nepveux. This chart was created by the Farm Bureau to illustrate the first seven weeks of the 2018/2019 marketing year, when sales officially started being inked. The lack of orders from the Chinese can easily be seen.

Fast forward to July of 2019: The Farm Bureau did a follow-up chart to show the pace of soybean purchases for the 2018/2019 marketing year. With a month to go before the marketing year closes for the 2018/2019 harvest, China would have to *triple* the number of purchases to make up for the purchases it has not made since the start of the trade war.

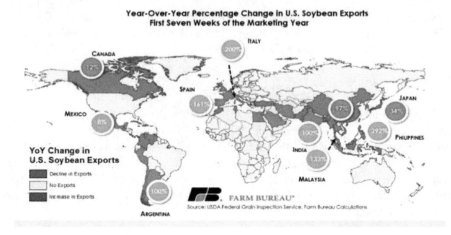

Farmers: CEOs of the Land

The business of agriculture extends beyond the field, and just like any industry it's all about relationships. Every year, U.S. producers and trade officials travel in early spring to existing buying countries, as well as countries of interest, to make new connections and fill those orders right after the harvest. They also set up a reciprocal trade missions for those buying countries to come to the United States to view the crops and ink deals. Traditionally, those missions are in September, when the crops are at their peak in the fields. That's when the deals for that batch of crops are officially made.

In April 2018, under the cloud of an all-out trade war, members of the U.S. Soybean Export Council (USEC) and the USDA Foreign Agriculture Service (FAS) traveled to China to meet with members of the Bean Product Committee China (BPCC). Despite the heightened tensions between the two countries, deals were made, and a mission of Chinese delegates agreed to travel in September to meet with North Dakota's bean, pea, and lentil growers. Additional delegations from India, Italy, and Spain were also scheduled.

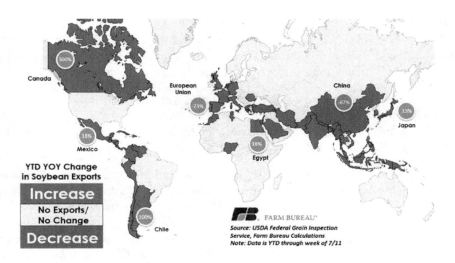

YTD YOY Change in Soybean Exports

Increase
No Exports/ No Change
Decrease

Source: USDA Federal Grain Inspection Service, Farm Bureau Calculations
Note: Data is YTD through week of 7/11

The North Dakota agriculture business community was expecting the 16-member Chinese trade mission for a visit from September 17 to 20. The North Dakota trade group was hoping for large orders to come out of those meetings. Farms were selected to bring the delegation to so the crop could be showcased. Then, a week before the set meeting, those expectations were crushed when the North Dakota Trade Office was notified the visit was canceled.

Simon Wilson, the executive director of the North Dakota Trade Office at that time, quickly called the BPCC to see if the meetings could be salvaged. Unfortunately, the optics of a Chinese trade delegation visit to America during the trade war in which both sides wanted to show strength was not what the Chinese wanted to telegraph. "They told us it was not the right political time to visit," Wilson said. "These meetings are about making deals and building relationships. The trips are not social calls."

Other country missions scheduled to visit the state called Wilson to tell him they too would be canceling their trade visits. Planned trade missions scheduled in September from Spain and Italy to buy lentil and pea crops were canceled as well. "The delegates explained to me that they were afraid of facing negative repercussions with their businesses at home if they came to the U.S.," said Wilson. "They said the reason behind the cancelation was there was too much uncertainty. But after all my years working with them, I took their comments [to mean that] if they came to America and purchased U.S. product it would be supporting the U.S. protectionist policies."

The U.S. agriculture industry produced a bumper crop in 2018, and their number one consumer and other buying countries closed their wallets. China purchased some of their fall season crop from other countries, like Canada. "The soybean from Canada is essentially the same quality of bean as in North Dakota," said Wilson. "There are no lines in the ground. It's the same soil and temperature. China knows that. Canada benefited from our pain."

For the Canadian soy farmer, 2018 was a boom year. Canadian soybean exports to China rose 80 percent to nearly 3.6 million tons in 2018 compared to 2017. "We've gone from a third of our exports going to China to over 60 percent in 2018," said Ron Davidson, executive director of Soy Canada.

In September 2018, at a time when the U.S. agriculture industry would usually be inking deals with China, the industry instead saw trade tensions escalate. Three key trade war moments happened during that month: On September 7, Trump threatened new tariffs on $267 billion more of Chinese imports; the Chinese canceled a trade meeting; and then, on September 24, the United States implemented a 10 percent tariff on $200 billion of Chinese imports. The administration said the rate would increase to 25 percent on January 1. China slapped back with its own set of retaliatory tariffs on $60 billion of U.S. goods. "The U.S. tariffs were the equivalent of the U.S. punching China in the nose," said Gibbs. "Why would they buy? Yes, every time my supplier punches me and tells me how he doesn't really need me, I always get warm and fuzzy and buy more product. *Not!*"

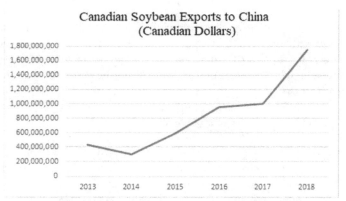

Source: Statistics Canada, 2018; CATSNET Analytics, 2018; Soy Canada Calculations, 2018. Updated: January 2019

US soya bean exports to China
2016-2019

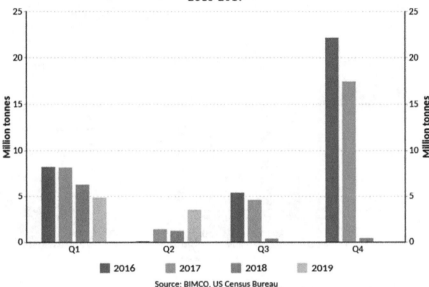

Source: BIMCO, US Census Bureau

Canada wasn't the only country China turned to. It also turned to Brazil. In the first eight months of 2018, Brazil exported 50.9 million tons of soybeans to China. That was a 15 percent increase, 6.8 million tons, compared to the 44.1 million tons exported during the same time frame in 2017. China's reaction to the increased tariffs levied by the Trump administration can be seen clearly in the October, November, and December cargo volumes. China hit back hard.

Because harvest periods for soybeans occur during different times of the year in North and South America, China does the bulk of its buying during the months of April through September from Brazil, and during November through March from the United States. This is when the soybeans are at their freshest in each country.

Traditionally, 80 percent of these countries' exports are purchased during these periods. But when trade tensions soured again, China turned its purchasing to Brazil and away from the United States.

In 2018, U.S. soybean exports to China totaled 16.6 million tons—barely *half* of 2017's 32.9 million tons. Not only were export sales impacted by the trade war, but soybean prices for the U.S. farmer were also decimated. The reality of the trade war and trade negotiations can be clearly documented. China was not at the negotiation table. They were playing hardball.

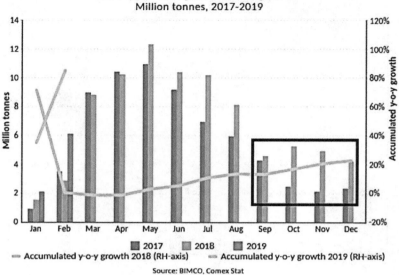

Brazilian soya bean exports
Million tonnes, 2017-2019

Legend: 2017 ■ 2018 ■ 2019
— Accumulated y-o-y growth 2018 (RH-axis) — Accumulated y-o-y growth 2019 (RH-axis)

Source: BIMCO, Comex Stat

US, BRAZIL SOYBEANS EXPORTS TO CHINA

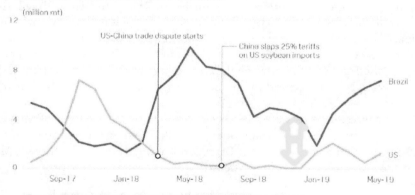

Source: Hellenic Shipping News, Brazil's MDIC, US Census Bureau

China raised prices on the American soybean so much that it killed orders. But on the flip side, it created an opportunity for America's soy competitors like Brazil to raise their soybean prices to just below the tariff price. "Our competitors were not only filling our orders," exclaimed Gibbs, "they were able to raise prices and make more money!"

USDA-FAS reported that U.S. soybean export bids in October 2018 averaged $325 per ton for U.S. soybeans that would be shipped out of the Gulf.

Meanwhile, soybeans from Paranaguá, Brazil, averaged $414 per ton, and Argentina Up River averaged $395 per ton. Average prices for both Brazil and Argentina increased.

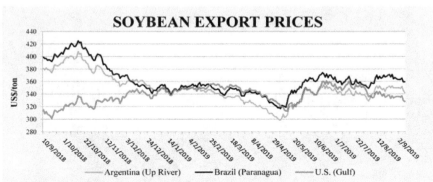

SOYBEAN EXPORT PRICES

Source: USDA, Foreign Agriculture Service, Oilseeds: World Markets and Trade, September 2019

As a result of China not buying, a tremendous surplus was weighing down the price of U.S. soybeans. In October 2018, the average U.S. soybean price was down $51 per ton compared with October 2017 ($376 per ton). For the same time period, the average prices for Brazil and Argentina were up $28 per ton and $17 per ton, respectively.

"We were looking at huge surpluses because we had agitated our largest customer," said Gibbs. "I explained the situation to someone the other day. It's like—if you're making $60,000 at your job and your boss comes out and says, you know, 'I made our biggest customer mad, and I hate to tell you this, but I'm going to take $20,000 off your paycheck. So as of tomorrow, you're only making $40,000. Okay?' That's what happened to U.S. farmers."

The China agriculture boycott expanded beyond the bean. Overall agriculture trade to China in 2018 was down more than 50 percent compared to 2017. Dairy products, pork, feed grains, and sorghum are just some of the products on China's lengthy tariff target. Before 2018, around 16 percent of all U.S. agriculture exports were delivered to China. But for 2019, the USDA forecast the number would be *half* that. "The longer this trade war continues, China will no longer be one of our top export markets," said John Newton, chief economist at American Farm Bureau Federation. "The ag industry has been successful at selling the products that would have gone to China to other countries, but the price is at a discount. Even with the new buyers, it isn't the same size as China purchases."

According to USDA data, in November 2018, China made no purchases of soybeans from the United States and just a small order in December.

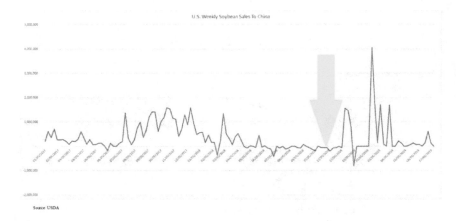

To fill its grain bins at home, China turned back to Brazil and purchased 4.39 million tons of soybeans that December instead of buying U.S. soybeans. It was a whopping 126 percent increase from 194 million tons purchased a year ago. The flow of trade showed that in 2018 China purchased more soybeans from Brazil than the year before. The fall season, which tends to be the U.S. export time, translated into a windfall for Brazil, particularly during the months of October, November, and December. U.S. soybean exports to China were down 98.3 percent during the peak months, and total exports to China over the 2018/2019 marketing year decreased to 68.7 percent.

The U.S.-China Business Council explained the fear of the repercussions of a long, drawn-out trade war. "It gives your customers the opportunity to find and buy a comparable product that is at a good—if not better—price. That is concerning," explained Erin Ennis. "Your competitor during this time period is able to *prove* that they are a reliable and worthy alternative. This makes it harder for you to get those customers back when things go back to somewhat normal." The Brazilian buys of soybeans are an example of this.

Trying to Fill the Near-Empty China Bucket

Because of the depressed price of U.S. soybeans, other countries, including Egypt, the Netherlands, Pakistan, Vietnam, Spain, Iran, and Taiwan, increased their imports of U.S. soybeans in 2018. In total, those seven countries have contributed to more than balancing out the 3.5 million decrease in Chinese imports in the first eight months of 2018 (compared to the same time frame in 2017).

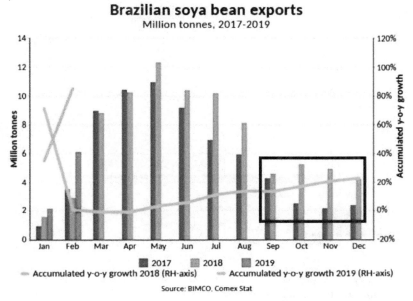

Brazilian soya bean exports
Million tonnes, 2017-2019

2017 2018 2019
Accumulated y-o-y growth 2018 (RH-axis) Accumulated y-o-y growth 2019 (RH-axis)

Source: BIMCO, Comex Stat

This buying trend has continued into 2019. "We have soybean exports to Mexico, which are up 16 percent; Netherlands, 64 percent; Egypt is up by 200 percent; and you have 50 percent more to Thailand," explained Newton. "Even Argentina, which does not typically buy from us, is up 150 percent. So you can go down the list. Just about everybody has purchased soybeans from the United States because of the discount."

Another market where the U.S. agriculture industry expanded its soybean exports in 2018 was the European Union. The U.S. soybean was attractive compared to the crop from Argentina and Uruguay, where supplies were tight as a result of drought and the premium price tag of the Brazilian soybean.

A New Year, but the Merry-Go-Round of Trade Talks Continues

In early 2019, the pledge to make agriculture purchases began again. "But so far that hasn't translated into beans shipped," said Newton. "About 200 million bushels have been loaded onto ships, but in a normal year, that number would be about 1 billion bushels."

US seaborne soya bean exports
largest importers, 2017-2018

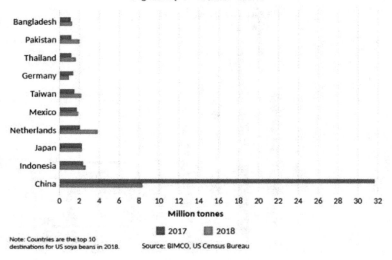

Note: Countries are the top 10 destinations for US soya beans in 2018.

Source: BIMCO, US Census Bureau

Unfortunately, because of the government shutdown over the U.S.-Mexico border wall funding, tracking the cargo in January 2019 was impossible. The USDA was closed, and the export data was delayed and could not be recorded and made public. The only news on the talks was being relayed through Twitter, which in the past had proven to be more a reflection of China's blustery promises than fact.

US soybean exports by destination

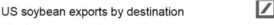

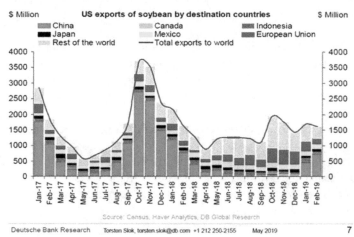

Source: Torsten Slok, Deutsche Bank

President Trump tweeted an update on talks after promises of soybean buys were announced by the Chinese.

Donald J. Trump ●
@realDonaldTrump

Following

Talks with China are going very well!

7:16 AM - 8 Jan 2019

18,655 Retweets **122,540** Likes

○ 21K   ↻ 19K   ♡ 123K   ✉

Weekly U.S. Soybean Sales to China

Date	Sales
01/03/2019	- 807,001
01/10/2019	-
01/17/2019	-
01/24/2019	-
01/31/2019	-
02/07/2019	-
02/14/2019	4,050,459

Source: BullPositions, USDA

But based on the volume of U.S. soybean orders to China, the truth of exports was contrary to the promises being made.

During the week of January 3, sales were down compared to that same week a year earlier. When the shutdown was over, in February, the USDA was back to work and compiled the purchases of those missing January weeks into the week of February 14. The lump of the combined sales created an artificial spike on the sales chart.

U.S. Weekly Soybean Sales To China

Source: USDA

The retaliatory pattern of buying Brazilian soybeans continued. This was predicted months before by maritime trade analysts like Peter Sand of BIMCO. China's negotiating strategy to not back down was evident in the cargo volumes. There is no spin. Brazilian soybean exports to China exploded in 2019. According to the vessel data and analysis by BIMCO, compared to the first two months of 2018, Brazilian exports employed an extra 47 Panamax loads (3.5 million tons). "The recent upturn in Panamax and Supramax earnings is likely to be linked to the start of the Brazilian soya bean exporting season. The large volumes being exported, in particular to China, have driven up the demand for the midsize dry bulk vessels," said Sand.

"Prior to the trade war, Chinese soybean purchases to the United States were *three* times what they are now," explained Sutter. While total U.S. soybean exports may have fallen 23.6 percent in the first 10 months of the 2018/2019 marketing season, exports to all destinations other than China have risen 31.9 percent, or 7.1 million tons, to reach 29.3 million tons.

"The E.U. and South and Central America have increased their purchases of U.S. soya beans, respectively growing 71.1 percent and 66 percent compared to the first 10 months of last season," explained Sand. "Several countries stand out for having massively grown their imports of soya beans from the U.S., such as Argentina and Spain, whose imports have grown enormously. Argentina imports grew 6,297.3 percent to reach 1.9 million tons, and Spain increased by 2620.5 percent to reach 1.7 million tons."

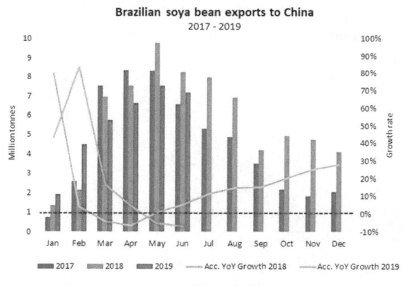

Brazilian soya bean exports to China
2017 - 2019

Source: BIMCO, Comex Stat

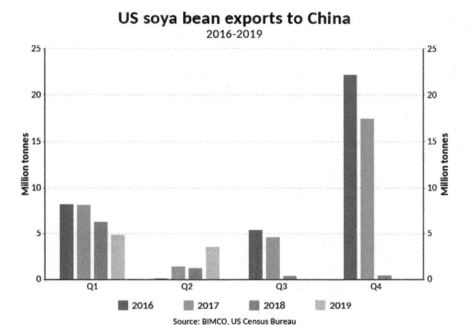

US soya bean exports to China
2016-2019

Source: BIMCO, US Census Bureau

An Ironic Twist on the Year of the Pig

If the trade war wasn't enough of a problem for soybean farmers, they faced an additional hurdle in 2019: the African swine fever. According to Rabobank, the pig flu decimated China's pork herd by 40 percent from the year before. The slashed population meant less demand for feed. And what do hogs eat? Soybeans. "The North Dakota trade delegation was in talks with the Chinese and planning a trip to China in April, but with the swine fever and rising of tensions again, our trip was canceled in late March," explained Wilson.

Instead of going to China, the North Dakota Trade Office sent a representative to meet with trade officials in Washington, D.C. "Due to the continued tariff and lack of any progress in trade talks in early 2019, the agri-businesses determined it was not the best investment to undertake the planned trade mission," Wilson said. "We conveyed our continued willingness to have trade partners. This was critical, as Canada had officials at the China trade events and were conveying their advantage and products to the Chinese buyers and industry personnel."

But while the soybean farmers had been hit with another whammy, the swine fever created an opportunity for the U.S. pig farmers. China's ailing pig population forced the Chinese to buy American pork. "It doesn't look like China is canceling many sales, and we are exporting well above last year," explained Nepveux.

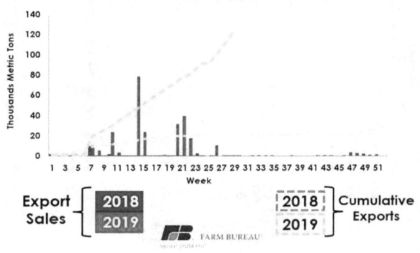

New Chapters in the Trade War

The lack of progress in talks and the supposed deal falling apart strained U.S.-China relations in the spring of 2019. Because the waiting period for announcing the intent of tariffs was long over, President Trump could initiate additional tariffs immediately. On May 5, he announced that the United States would increase tariffs from 10 percent to 25 percent on $200 billion of Chinese goods. It would be effective on May 10. China responded with its own set of retaliatory tariffs and announced that the country was producing an "unreliable entities list" that would identify foreign companies that do not obey Chinese market rules, cut off supply for noncommercial reasons, violate contacts, or severely damage Chinese companies' interests.

The June G-20 meeting between Xi Jinping and President Trump proved to yield more lopsided intent and more action—versus additional rhetoric—on the United States' part than from the Chinese. The United States agreed to ease restrictions on the Chinese telecom giant Huawei Technologies and to not impose any new tariffs. China agreed to purchase U.S. farm products—but did not specify the amount. The United States followed through on its Huawei and tariff pledge. Did China hold up its part of the bargain? No.

Data released by the USDA on July 11 shows that China *slowed* its purchases of American agriculture products following the G-20 meeting. China reduced purchases of U.S. soybeans by 79 percent to 127,800 metric tons, which is equal to approximately two cargoes. Pork purchases didn't fare well either, with China buying only 76 tons versus the 10,400 tons purchased in June. The lack of cargoes speaks volumes.

But China did expand its buying in Russia. On July 25, just six days before Treasury Secretary Mnuchin and U.S. Trade Representative Lighthizer met in Shanghai for another round of trade talks, the Chinese customs administration started allowing soybean imports from all parts of Russia, expanding from five regions in eastern Russia near the border of China. They also announced that Chinese farmers were going to Russia to grow soybeans. In 2018, China imported more than 800,000 tons—an increase of 64.7 percent. These deals will further alter the flow of trade and shed light on China's intentions of broadening its soybean production base.

"Additional acreage developed and harvested by other countries takes away from the United States agriculture industry," explained Gibbs. "China sending farmers to Russia to grow soybeans is another move of replacing U.S."

After the soybean expansion in Russia, it came as no surprise when, after the follow-up meeting between trade delegations from the United States and China, the Chinese indicated they were in this war for the long-term. "The two sides discussed increasing purchase of U.S. farm products, and the U.S. side agreed to create favorable conditions for it. They will hold future talks," Chinese Foreign Ministry spokeswoman Hua Chunying said, without adding more detail.

In response to a question about a tweet by President Trump on China not being serious about making a deal, Hua said, "I believe it doesn't make any sense for the U.S. to exercise its campaign of maximum pressure at this time. It's pointless to tell others to take medication when you're the one who is sick."

The tit-for-tat trade war between the United States and China was ratcheted up on August 1 when President Trump announced a 10 percent tariff on the remaining $300 billion in Chinese products, effective September 1. The reason? China had not followed through on its promises to buy agricultural products.

China responded sharply. "We don't want to fight, but we aren't afraid to," Hua said at a regular news briefing. She said the Trump administration should "abandon its illusions, correct mistakes, and return to consultations based on equality and mutual respect."

71

When the tariff was announced, I was not surprised. The truth in the cargo had been a red flag indicating China's true intentions since the start of negotiations. The rhetoric from the president talking about China's lack of sincerity in promising to purchase U.S. agriculture products was another telltale sign.

Donald J. Trump ✔
@realDonaldTrump

China is doing very badly, worst year in 27 - was supposed to start buying our agricultural product now - no signs that they are doing so. That is the problem with China, they just don't come through. Our Economy has become MUCH larger than the Chinese Economy is last 3 years....

7:09 AM · Jul 30, 2019 · Twitter for iPhone

19K Retweets **94.8K** Likes

In less than 24 hours, before the global community could fully digest the news, reports were out that the president was going to make another trade announcement—this time regarding the E.U.

Flanked by beef industry representatives and his trade officials, President Trump signed a deal to lower trade barriers in Europe that would expand U.S. beef exports. The agreement, according to the USTR, would potentially triple U.S. beef exports to $420 million from $150 million. "This is a tremendous victory for American farmers, ranchers, and of course, European consumers," President Trump said as he unveiled the deal at the White House.

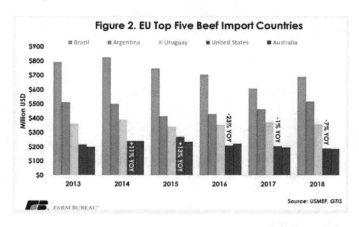

Figure 2. EU Top Five Beef Import Countries

The president said this deal was "one more step in giving [U.S. farmers] a level playing field" in trade. "In year one, duty-free American beef exports to the E.U. will increase by 46 percent. Over seven years, they will increase by another 90 percent," he said. "Overall, duty-free beef exports will rise from $150 million to $420 million [a year]."

President Trump added that the deal was a part of the administration's goal to open markets like Japan, Morocco, Australia, and Tunisia. He also praised his administration's efforts to help the farmers impacted by the trade war with China by distributing a second round of aid.

"When our farmers became victims of unjustified retaliatory tariffs from China and other countries, we provided $28 billion over two years in relief," he said. U.S. farmers "are the first to be targeted" by other countries, "but we take that target off their back."

The subject of the aid does not sit well with many farmers. While the trade groups blast out press releases thanking the administration for offering the assistance, the farmers themselves speak out on television or other forms of media. While the farmers' comments have been condemned as "fake news," there is nothing fake about their fears and emotions.

Cindy Brown, president of CV Bean, is a seventh-generation Wisconsin kidney bean processor and supplier who found her company in the middle of the U.S.-E.U. trade war. The 28-nation European Union imposed over $3 billion in tariffs on products like whiskey, peanut butter, and kidney beans, along with Harley Davidson motorcycles.

The E.U. was CV Bean's largest international market, with an annual value of $25 million, accounting for 60 percent of the company's export sales. Suddenly, that lucrative market was no more. "The bailout on dry beans, peas, lentils, and chickpeas was called 'trade mitigation,' which meant the government purchased the pulses for domestic feeding programs," explained Brown. "But there was no cash bailout for pulses like soybeans. Trade is far better than aid. Give us back the opportunity to sell our products. Also, this bailout does not help the national deficit. It only contributes to it."

"President Trump continues to hail the farmers as patriots for following him into this trade war," Gibbs said. "He is using the word 'patriot' to shut us up, because if we speak out against the tariffs, he can call us unpatriotic," he continued. "That's not true. You know what 'patriotic' is for agriculture? For me, it's to keep my business viable. You know why? Because farmers buy things that are manufactured with U.S. steel and aluminum. We also buy local fuel and supplies. We take care of the local hardware store, the local veterinary, we take care of the state universities. Agriculture supports *all* of this. So if the farmers go down, we are in trouble. Being patriotic is not to take one in shorts so that the president can stand up and beat up on China and make his base happy."

Donald J. Trump ✔
@realDonaldTrump

Our great Patriot Farmers will be one of the biggest beneficiaries of what is happening now. Hopefully China will do us the honor of continuing to buy our great farm product, the best, but if not your Country will be making up the difference based on a very high China buy......

7:29 AM · May 14, 2019 · Twitter for iPhone

15.5K Retweets   **77.3K** Likes

Donald J. Trump ✔
@realDonaldTrump

....This money will come from the massive Tariffs being paid to the United States for allowing China, and others, to do business with us. The Farmers have been "forgotten" for many years. Their time is now!

7:29 AM · May 14, 2019 · Twitter for iPhone

13.4K Retweets   **67.8K** Likes

Beyond the Bean

Soybeans, lentils, and chickpeas are just some of the agricultural products being tariffed. Cherries and other fruits like grapes and apples, meats, and even lobster have been clobbered by the retaliatory tariffs. The state of Washington, the nation's largest cherry producer, saw exports to China cut in half.

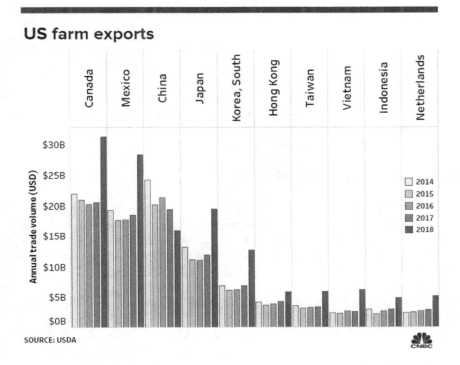

While China has closed its doors to the U.S. product, U.S. agricultural exports have found a home in Vietnam, where exports were up 20 percent in the first half of 2019 compared to the same time frame in 2018, with a 70 percent increase specifically in fruits and vegetables.

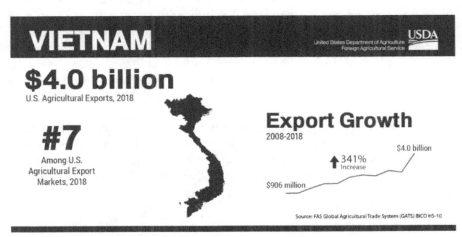

The Future

With another round of tariffs set to hit China at the beginning of another agriculture marketing year, the future of agriculture sales with China and the trickle-down impact they can have on the U.S. economy is muddy. "Agriculture contributes about 1.5 trillion dollars to U.S. GDP. That's about 6 percent of the U.S. economy," said Newton. "If a farmer has less money, that means he can hire fewer people and purchase less equipment. In the end, that means he injects less reinvestment in the community."

Newton's words are an echo of Gibbs's.

The trade war with China, because of its size, has dominated the headlines, but the United States is also in trade wars with other countries and regions. Undeterred by a dismal 2018/2019 season because of the tariffs on kidney beans, Brown attended the AnuFoods show in Brazil and spoke with buyers from around the world in hopes of inking deals for her crop. "We learned the U.S. product is still too expensive, and unless there is a product shortage in Brazil, Argentina, or Central America, there will be no opportunity to compete," Brown said. "Farmers in Brazil, Argentina, and Central America are also increasing their production to meet the demands from the non-tariffed countries. We continue to look for new markets, but the barrier to entry is high in terms of freight and pricing."

Brown said if history can be any guide, tariffs have already proven to alter the flow of trade and hurt the U.S. agriculture industry. "The effects of the Soviet Grain Embargo in 1980 changed the face of U.S. agriculture. Argentina and Brazil were quick to fill that void of U.S. wheat and corn by increasing production," she said. "They succeeded, and that route of trade was changed forever. Now the steel and aluminum tariffs have created an open invitation for farmers outside the United States to start growing kidney beans. It won't take many seasons to change the global production of kidney beans. We have already seen it happen."

"With a worsening relationship between the U.S. and China, this trade is unlikely to return to previous levels any time soon, if it ever does," warned Sand. "For any hope of the trade returning to previous levels, a trade agreement will need to be reached between the nations, and even then, once a market has disappeared, there is no guarantee that it will return."

Big Beautiful Deal?

The China October trade mission was closely watched by the markets as headlines reported impasses and the Chinese trade team trip being cut short increased investor anxiety. Market futures swung widely. The body language of China's Vice Premier Liu He and the U.S. trade team was a subject of discussion. Then, word of an agreement started to emerge, and the markets ignited in a blaze of green glory.

Finally, the markets received the news they were hoping for. In an Oval Office presser on October 11, 2019, President Trump, with Ambassador Lighthizer, Secretary Mnuchin, and China's Vice Premier Liu He in the room, announced the framework of a trade deal with China.

The President explained that the agreement was not yet in written form, it would take three to four weeks to draw up, and it "could" be signed when President Xi and he met at the Asian-Pacific Leaders summit in Chile in mid-November. This agreement was not the big agreement President Trump originally pushed. Instead of one big deal, it would be broken up into a series of mini deals. President Trump called the agreement the "greatest and biggest deal ever."

Donald J. Trump ✔
@realDonaldTrump

The deal I just made with China is, by far, the greatest and biggest deal ever made for our Great Patriot Farmers in the history of our Country. In fact, there is a question as to whether or not this much product can be produced? Our farmers will figure it out. Thank you China!

10:09 AM · Oct 12, 2019 · Twitter for iPhone

25.6K Retweets **109.9K** Likes

President Trump explained that the outline of the phase-one partial trade agreement would include China pledging to make purchases of $40 billion to $50 billion in agriculture goods. The number was hailed as historic, and the president said the farmers would need to buy more land and John Deeres to meet the demand. But let's pull the veil off this claim and put it into perspective with the truth of the containers.

In the press conference, Secretary Mnuchin said that the $40 billion to $50 billion in agriculture purchases would be made over a two-year period. So let's go back to the trade data and see what the Chinese were buying in agriculture products in a two-year period *before* the trade war.

According to the Farm Bureau, in 2016 China made $25,459,000 in agriculture buys; in 2017, $24,348,000. Those two years combined totaled $49.8 billion. So the new deal that was announced would get the agriculture community back to where it once was. Nothing groundbreaking when you look at the historical data. What this trade flow data does show is the trade destruction the trade war created. Based on the same Farm Bureau data, the Chinese purchased $13,420,000 in 2018.[59]

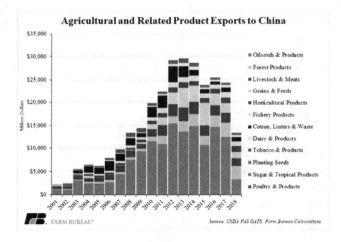

"So let me get this straight, we should be breaking out the champagne for the *promise* of purchases that would get us back to where were once *were?*" questioned Gibbs. "How gullible and desperate does the President think we farmers are? We know how much China was buying before this mess. This deal is not huge. In fact, it's status quo! We were told we were patriots because of the financial pain this trade war has inflicted on this industry because this was a war over intellectual property. Where is the big deal on that? Not to mention, we've heard about these grand gesture purchases before. I'll be keeping my champagne on ice, thank you."

---

[59]   Farm Bureau Calculations, USDA, FAS GATS

CHAPTER FOUR

Energy Blackout

The pattern in the flow of trade has shown China's intent to wean itself off of the United States as a supplier not only of soybeans but other products and commodities as well. This includes U.S. energy. Compared to soybeans and other products that are grown in limited areas, the supply of energy is far more abundant, which gives China flexibility in cutting out the United States.

In 2018, China became the world's largest LNG importer. Australia, Russia, and Qatar were the main suppliers of LNG to the energy-thirsty country. This was a market the United States desperately wanted to tap into. With the rapid growth of LNG exports, the United States officially became the world's third largest LNG exporter in 2019 and is expected to stay in that slot, behind Australia and Qatar, in 2019/2020.[60]

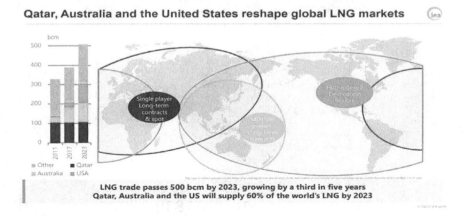

Qatar, Australia and the United States reshape global LNG markets

LNG trade passes 500 bcm by 2023, growing by a third in five years
Qatar, Australia and the US will supply 60% of the world's LNG by 2023

With more energy export infrastructure being constructed in the United States, the Energy Information Administration (EIA) is projecting that the country will become the largest gas producer in the world by 2024.

---

[60] "U.S. LNG Exports to Europe Increase Amid Declining Demand and Spot LNG Prices in Asia," U.S. Energy Information Administration, July 29, 2019

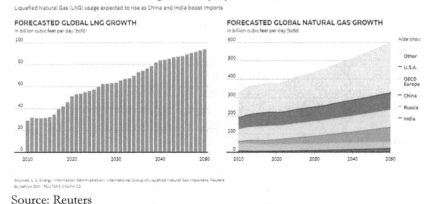

LNG share of world natural gas trade projected to rise

Liquefied Natural Gas (LNG) usage expected to rise as China and India boost imports

FORECASTED GLOBAL LNG GROWTH
In billion cubic feet per day (bcfd)

FORECASTED GLOBAL NATURAL GAS GROWTH
In billion cubic feet per day (bcfd)

Source: Reuters

In the crude oil arena, the United States was fifth in 2018.

Exporter	US$ Value	% of Total Exports	
Saudi Arabia:	$182.5 billion	(16.1%)	
Russia:	$129 billion	(11.4%)	
Iraq:	$91.7 billion	(8.1%)	
Canada:	$66.9 billion	(5.9%)	
United Arab Emirates:	$58.4 billion	(5.2%)	
Kuwait:	$51.7 billion	(4.6%)	*By value, the listed 15*
Iran:	$50.8 billion	(4.5%)	*countries accounted for*
United States:	$48.3 billion	(4.3%)	*80.4% of all crude oil*
Nigeria:	$43.6 billion	(3.8%)	*exported in 2018.*
Kazakhstan:	$37.8 billion	(3.3%)	
Angola:	$36.5 billion	(3.2%)	
Norway:	$33.3 billion	(2.9%)	
Libya:	$26.7 billion	(2.4%)	
Mexico:	$26.5 billion	(2.3%)	
Venezuela:	$26.4 billion	(2.3%)	

Top 15 Crude Oil Exporters 2018 (in US$)

Source: World's Top Exports

China's View on Energy Trade

When Xi Jinping was elected President of the People's Republic of China on March 14, 2013, China's energy consumption per unit of GDP was 2.5 times the world average.[61] It outpaced United States energy consumption by 2.9 times

---

[61]   Chen Yongjie, "China Needs to Slow Down," *The Economic Observer*, April 4, 2013

and was 4.5 times higher than Japan's. China also faced a growing problem of air pollution because of its dependence on coal energy.

Total primary energy consumption in China by fuel type, 2012

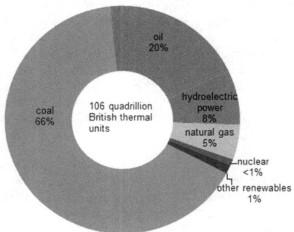

eia Note: Total may not equal 100% due to independent rounding. Includes only commercial fuel sources and does not account for biomass used outside of power generation.
Source: U.S. Energy Information Administration.

A week after his election, Xi traveled to Russia to meet with President Vladimir Putin to discuss energy and security issues. Russia was an essential partner in the growth and fortification of the Chinese Belt and Road Initiative's Maritime Silk Road and Ice Silk Road. Energy would be a large benefactor. Russia and China reportedly agreed to build the Ice Silk Road along the Northern Sea Route in the Arctic in order to connect Russia's internal waters to the new shipping route, providing key access and faster transportation of Russia's LNG to Asia. These two roads were a win-win for both countries. China would have access to Russian energy, and Russia would have faster access to Asia. This meeting with Putin was just the beginning of Xi's plan to expand energy relationships.

The Xi administration was focused on energy reform as part of its long-term plan of domestic sustainable growth. Every five years, the Chinese government lays out its economic plan at the major policy meeting called the Third Plenum. In November 2013, Xi outlined his broad principles for economic reform in China. His ultimate goal was to balance and fortify the economy by shifting away from dependence on exports and increasing domestic production and consumption. One of the key drivers highlighted in China's 13th Five Year Plan on oil and gas was the construction of infrastructure. By increasing self-sufficiency, China would have a country-centered trading network. This goes back to the ultimate goal of the Belt and Road Initiative: having a strong centralized trading network within China.

In order to build and foster an environment of growth, the Xi administration wanted to move toward a market system based on price, and, through competition, create efficient energy technology innovation. To tackle China's problem with air pollution, larger clean energy investments would also be made in renewable energy (solar, nuclear, wind, biomass-geothermal, and hydro-power). To fast-track these clean energy projects, China streamlined the approval process, relaxed price controls, and introduced policies to create more energy infrastructure to connect supply and demand centers. Billions of yuan in subsidies were allocated.

In his June 2014 speech delivered at the Central Financial and Economic Leading Group, Xi laid out his "energy revolution." He stressed that this energy revolution was vital to the prosperity and development of China. His plan focused on three core initiatives: reducing energy consumption, increasing energy supply, and improving energy efficiency. All future energy policy decisions would be based on those fundamentals.

China's insatiable appetite for all things energy made it an attractive and very lucrative market for energy exporters. Xi used the country's status as the number one consumer of energy as leverage in dealmaking. Xi declared, "We must judge the situation and take advantage of the situation to find a way to adapt to the energy trend."[62] The trade footprint of China's energy has expanded under this philosophy. When China started to import LNG in 2017, it received natural gas from four nations. By 2018, China's LNG import portfolio had diversified.

This growth is a reflection of Xi's mandate to diverse transport route suppliers to offset any supply shocks or dependence on a specific country for their energy needs. Also fueling China's natural gas consumption was the Blue Skies policy, which aims to improve air quality by moving residents' power off of "dirty coal" to gas or electricity for heating. On April 2017, the National Development and Reform Commission (NDRC) and the National Energy Administration (NEA) released a paper on China titled "Energy Supply and Consumption Revolution

---

[62] Xi Jinping delivered a speech stressing the active promotion of energy production and consumption revolution, June 14, 2014. Sina Finance, finance.sina.com.cn/money/fund/20140614/141319413598.shtml

Strategy." The mix of energy use, climate change commitments, and energy consumption were pivotal points in the plan.

Country	Where China Imports its Natural Gas		
	CY 2018 Import Share, LNG and Pipeline (%)	CY 2018 Import Volume, LNG and Pipeline (Bcm/Y)	CY 2018 Import Volume, LNG and Pipeline (Bcf/Y)
Turkmenistan	27.4%	33.30	3.22
Australia	26.4%	32.09	3.10
Qatar	10.5%	12.70	1.23
Malaysia	6.5%	7.87	0.76
Indonesia	5.5%	6.71	0.65
Uzbekistan	5.2%	6.30	0.61
Kazakhstan	4.4%	5.40	0.52
Papua New Guinea	2.7%	3.29	0.32
United States	2.5%	2.98	0.29
Myanmar	2.4%	2.90	0.28
Nigeria	1.2%	1.52	0.15
Russian Federation	1.1%	1.29	0.12
Other Africa	0.9%	1.09	0.10
Other Europe	0.7%	0.87	0.08
Oman	0.6%	0.68	0.07
Angola	0.5%	0.66	0.06
Trinidad/Tobago	0.4%	0.52	0.05
Brunei	0.2%	0.28	0.03
Norway	0.2%	0.25	0.02
Egypt	0.2%	0.25	0.02
Other Asia Pacific	0.2%	0.21	0.02
Algeria	0.1%	0.09	0.01
Peru	0.1%	0.09	0.01
Other Americas	0.0%	0.00	0.00
Total imports	100.0%	121.35	11.73

Source: ClearView Energy Partners, LLC BP data

As trade war tensions increased in August 2018, Xi called for China to increase its domestic energy security. China's state energy plants announced they would be expanding domestic oil and gas exploration as well as natural gas supplies. Even with slower economic growth, China's energy demand rose by 4.3 percent in 2018. It was the highest recorded since 2012.[63]

Despite China's goal of increasing energy production in order to be more self-sufficient, imports were still greatly needed to fill the production gap. According to the National Bureau of Statistics of China, imports made up 45.3 percent of the country's natural gas demand in 2018, and China's reliance on imported gas

---

[63] "BP Statistical Review of World Energy," 2019

is estimated to rise 50 percent by 2020.[64] Before the trade war, U.S. LNG exports quadrupled from 2016 to 2017 and made up 15 percent of China's LNG imports.[65]

The mix of energy sources has continued to evolve in China. Over the past decade, while coal is still China's primary source of energy, its share has slowly declined. In 2018, coal consumption decreased to 58 percent, from 60 percent in 2017 and a whopping 72 percent 10 years ago.[66] Gas consumption increased by 18 percent in 2018.[67]

According to the 2019 BP Energy Outlook, China's natural gas demand is forecasted to soar by 166 percent between 2017 and 2040. That would lead China's import dependence to increase from 38 percent in 2017 to 43 percent in 2040. It is an ironic twist to China's energy footprint. In an effort to grow as a nation, its dependence on foreign energy needs to increase.

One of the key components of China's growth is infrastructure. The two international gas pipelines, the China-Myanmar and China–Central Asia, are the only two international gas channels to bring fuel into China. They collectively transport 15 percent of the annual national gas consumption and 40 percent of the country's national gas imports a year.

On the oil front, the Chinese government announced plans in March 2019 to create a new national pipeline, called China Pipelines Corp., which would take control over the transportation and pipelines from the country's national oil companies (NOC): Sinopec, Asia's biggest refiner; China National Petroleum Corporation (CNPC); and China National Offshore Oil Corporation (CNOOC). CNPC operates 53 oil and gas projects in 20 countries involved in the Belt and Road Initiative.

The synergies of President Trump and Xi's energy plans cannot be ignored. Energy is a pivotal component in both countries' economies. While China continues with its plan of energy self-sufficiency, the country has reshaped the global energy markets with its enormous appetite, and the world energy importers all want that dominant market share.

---

[64] "China Country Commercial Guide – Oil and Gas," export.gov, July 30, 2019
[65] Victoria Zaretskaya, "U.S. Liquefied Natural Gas Exports Quadrupled in 2017," Today in Energy, U.S. Energy Information Administration, March 27, 2018
[66] "BP Statistical Review of World Energy," 2019
[67] "BP Statistical Review of World Energy," 2019

U.S.-China Energy Relations Before the Trade War

Growing America's energy resources and making the country a top exporter started as campaign promises and are now part of President Trump's economic agenda. In April 2017, President Trump met Xi for the first time, at the U.S. president's private Palm Beach club, Mar-a-Lago. Stemming out of that summit, Xi agreed to a 100-day plan that would boost U.S. exports to trim the U.S. trade deficit. Also as part of that deal, China pledged to buy U.S. LNG.

In November 2017, President Trump visited China on his first state visit, during which 37 major deals amounting to $253.4 billion were signed between U.S. and Chinese companies. Many of the deals that were made were memorandums of understanding (MOU).[68] In one MOU, the state-owned energy and chemical company Sinopec, the Bank of China, and the sovereign wealth fund China Investment Corporation agreed to join the Alaska Gasline Development Corporation's LNG megaproject, which is composed of three large pieces: a gas treatment plant on the North Slope, an 800 mile pipeline down to Cook Inlet, and a liquefaction plant in Nikisi.

Donald J. Trump @
@realDonaldTrump

It was a great honor to have President Xi Jinping and Madame Peng Liyuan of China as our guests in the United States. Tremendous...

10:50 AM · Apr 8, 2017 · Twitter for iPhone

9.3K Retweets **61K** Likes

Donald J. Trump @ @realDonaldTrump · Apr 8, 2017
Replying to @realDonaldTrump
...goodwill and friendship was formed, but only time will tell on trade.

3.4K   6.3K   44.1K

"I take notice of MOUs, but I generally don't get excited until sales and purchase agreements start getting signed," said Kevin Book, managing director of ClearView Energy Partners, LLC. "An MOU is like a first or second date. There's a lot of terrain to cover before the final investment decision [FID], and

---

[68]   A memorandum of understanding is a formal document describing the agreement between two or more parties that was reached during negotiations. This is *not* a legally binding document. It is about *intentions* of all parties moving forward.

even at the moment of the FID, companies are standing on the altar looking out at a lifetime commitment. 'No' can still be the answer."

This was not the first such deal made on the Alaska project. The project was originally pursued by the consortium of BP, ConocoPhillips, and ExxonMobil, but they later pulled out because the economics of the project did not make sense; the estimated $45 billion to $60 billion price tag would not be able to be recouped with the low price of LNG.

"North Slope gas has needed a market for a long time, and China needs gas for the foreseeable future," said Book. "It sounds good on the surface, but even when molecules line up with markets, economics and politics can get in the way. That's how it turned out. Project costs in the high double-digit billions of dollars made for fragile economics, and betting on China for financing and offtake at the dawn of a trade war seemed like the definition of fragile politics. The outcome did not surprise us."

In February 2018, as trade tensions were increasing between the United States and China with the introduction of tariffs, a new chapter of U.S. LNG began.[69] LNG supplier Cheniere Energy inked the nation's first long-term LNG deal with China National Petroleum Corporation. The agreement guaranteed the purchase of 1.2 million tons of U.S. LNG per year, with incremental increases from 2018 to 2023. The deal was months in the making. A Cheniere representative was picked as a member of President Trump's envoy for that November trip. The deal was then negotiated as part of the state visit.

"The existing deals pay for infrastructure that's in use today," said Book. "It's *tomorrow*'s deals that pay for the next wave of U.S. facilities. If U.S. companies can't sign long-term sales and purchase agreements with China, which is the world's biggest growth market, it's going to make it harder to pay for the next wave."

U.S. LNG exports to China were the highest that year in the month of April. A total of 0.58 billion cubic feet per day of U.S. LNG was imported by the Chinese. After that, the stress of the trade war started to slowly wear down LNG purchases.

---

[69] On January 17, 2018, U.S. imposed tariffs on all imported washing machines and solar panels; on March 8, 2018, the 232 tariffs on steel and aluminum imposed.

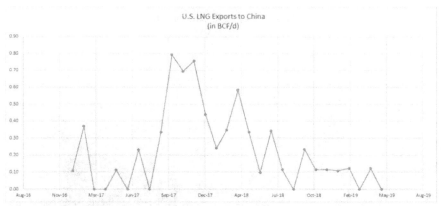

Source: U.S. Department of Energy, ClearView Energy Partners

China Crude Reality

While Russia was the number one exporter of crude to China in 2018, the U.S. was the fastest growing supplier: up by 1,994 percent in 2018 since 2016.[70] China's new refinery capacity and stockpiling combined with a decline in domestic oil production fueled the import increase. According to the International Trade Administration, 80 percent of China's crude supply is expected to be imported by 2030. That would create a huge opportunity for U.S. crude exports.

U.S. crude oil exports to China were strong until July 2018. An unexpected drop in exports rattled the oil markets.

Oil may not have been on any official tariff list for China, but the chatter energy researchers heard was troubling. When the tit-for-tat trade war officially began in July 2018 and the tariffs went into effect, China was already silently targeting crude.

"There were rumors that Chinese buyers, led by the world's top tanker charter, Unipec, were staying away," explained Peter Sand of BIMCO. "Unfortunately, you could not verify. China started keeping its oil import data closer than ever before. Up until March of 2018, we had a good idea of where they were buying crude, and then it all stopped. China now only releases their import volumes, not sources of their imports."

---

[70]   U.S. Exports, China – Oil and Gas, July 30, 2019

Seaborne US crude oil exports in volumes and tonne miles
2016-2019

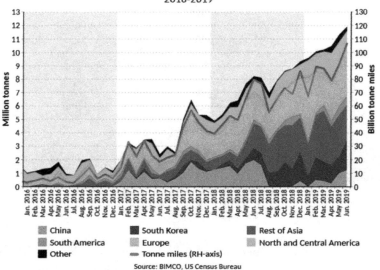

China	South Korea	Rest of Asia
South America	Europe	North and Central America
Other	Tonne miles (RH-axis)	

Source: BIMCO, US Census Bureau

Note: On 18 December 2015 Congress lifted the 41 year old ban on crude oil exports.

"For the first seven months of 2018, China imported an average of 377,700 barrels of U.S. crude per day, according to U.S. Energy Department figures, surpassing Canada as the biggest foreign buyer of U.S. barrels," Sand said. Then, in August 2018, U.S. crude oil exports dropped to zero. "Chinese buyers completely stopped their imports because of the trade war," said Sand. "The data of the zero U.S. crude oil exports proved the rumors true." Another zero month was recorded for September 2018.

Because of the travel distance by tanker, you need to work backward to figure out exactly when the trades—or, in these cases, the *no* trades—were made. U.S. oil tankers take about one to one and a half months to reach China. When you factor that travel time into the timing of the no buys it makes sense: The zero exports in August would have been around the threat announced by Beijing in June 2018 that they were planning to impose a 25 percent tariff on crude oil imports to China. The no exports in September can be explained by the tariffs that were already underway in late July. With the crude tariff threat announced by the Chinese, both state-owned Unipec (the trading arm of Sinopec) and the independent Chinese crude importers did not want to risk having a vessel full of crude on the open water if tariffs were imposed. Ultimately, the Chinese did not follow through on their threat.

US crude oil exports
2017-2018

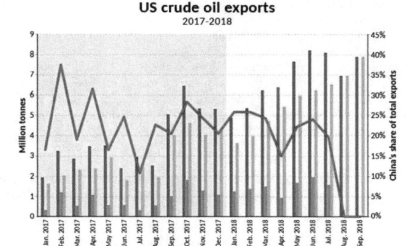

World total ■ China ▨ World total (excl. China) ▨ China's share of total exports (RH-axis)

Source: BIMCO, US Census Bureau

With the lack of import visibility in the Chinese data, maritime trade experts like Sand had to wait to review the U.S. Customs data to get a clear picture of what was happening in the flow of the crude oil trade. That data was delayed by two months, but what it ultimately showed was that Unipec, one of the largest buyers of U.S. oil, had stopped buying oil in August and hadn't return for the rest of the year. But that does not mean U.S. exports didn't flow into China at all. Smaller cargoes of crude oil were imported into China in November by independent refineries.

"The trade war between the U.S. and China is now impacting trade in both tariffed and some non-tariffed goods, with both countries looking elsewhere for alternative buyers and sellers," said Sand. So where exactly were those alternative buyers and sellers?

The Expansion in Crude Plumbing

Unlike soybeans, crude oil does not have a limited customer base. Despite the shock of no crude oil deliveries to China in August and September and the nominal purchases for the rest of the year, U.S. crude oil exports continued to increase every month.

South Korea purchased the oil that would have gone to China. In fact, South Korea's crude oil purchases rose 318 percent compared to 2017. That almost made South Korea the largest buyer of crude in 2018. It was a narrow second to Canada. Only one million tons separated the two countries: Canada with 12 million tons to South Korea's 11 million tons.

The increase of volumes continued through the end of 2018. "Volumes for the full year totaled 88.5 million tons," explained Sand. "That was 96 percent higher than the 45.1 million tons exported in 2017. That was good news for the crude oil tanker sector, because it meant more tankers were needed. An additional 145 very large crude carrier loads or 289 Suezmax vessels were used in 2018 compared to 2017."

A very large crude carrier (VLCC) can transport 2 million barrels of crude oil. Suezmax vessels are half the size of VLCCs and can carry about 800,000 to about 1 million barrels.

The bullish flow of U.S. crude oil exports continued to set new record highs in 2019. In the month of January, 9.6 million ton miles were recorded, according to BIMCO analysis. "Exports rose in January on the back of increased sales to Europe, which were up from 2.7 million tons in December to 4.8 million tons in January," explained Sand.

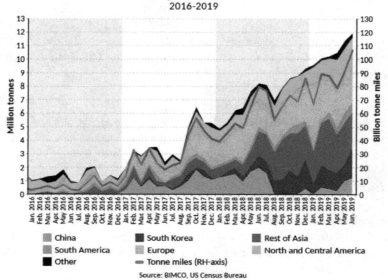

Seaborne US crude oil exports in volumes and tonne miles
2016-2019

Source: BIMCO, US Census Bureau

Note: On 18 December 2015 Congress lifted the 41 year old ban on crude oil exports.

Following the flow of the trade pipes, the Netherlands took the top spot as the largest importer of U.S. crude oil, knocking out Canada in January. South Korea, which was the biggest importer of seaborne crude exports in 2018, fell to fourth place. Why the sudden drop for South Korea? A trade war. The slump in U.S. exports to South Korea in January was driven not by the U.S.-China trade war but by South Korea's own trade conflict with Japan: the centuries-old dispute over reparations for historical abuses during Japanese colonial rule of the Korean Peninsula. This bitter battle has escalated with sanctions and its own set of trade war tensions. This different trade war shows the trickle-down impact trade wars can have on other countries. U.S. exports to South Korea precipitously fell from 2.25 million tons in December to 0.86 million tons in January.

So which countries did China turn to in order to replace its U.S. crude imports? Iran, Nigeria, and Angola. "Ironically, the West African crude was the crude the U.S. used to buy before the shale revolution," said Sand.

Unipec's absence added to the massive decrease in maritime trade miles. China was the largest importer of U.S. crude oil until the summer of 2018, accounting for 23.3 percent of all seaborne exports. In January 2019, no U.S. crude was imported into China.

"Although small volumes of U.S. crude oil were sent to China in November and December, following a three-month pause in the trade, BIMCO did not take this as a sign that tensions between the two countries had eased, and was therefore not surprised by the lack of exports to China in January," said Sand. "A positive outcome from the ongoing trade negotiations is needed if this trade is to return to levels seen before the trade war."

But the tanker industry makes money on distance, and the massive decrease in Chinese and South Korean exports in January ate into the industry's bottom line. Ton miles dropped because the sailing distances were shorter.

"The importance of Asia cannot be underestimated when considering how U.S. crude oil exports impact the shipping industry," explained Sand. "In 2018, 71.5 percent of the ton mile demand generated by U.S. crude oil exports originated from exports to Asia. The sudden drop in exports to Asia in January was therefore particularly harmful to the crude oil tanker shipping industry. VLCC earnings rose to $53,121 per day in November, when vessels are being fixed for the following month, before falling again in January when ton mile demand dropped."

The decrease from Asia continued into 2019. Exports to Asia dropped to 3.7 million tons from 5.5 million tons in March. According to BIMCO research in the first four months of 2019, exports to Asia generated 12.2 times as many ton miles compared to exports to North and Central America. "The longer the sailing distance, the more valuable the trade is to the shipping industry. Demand for shipping is measured in ton miles, not just the amount of crude being transported," said Sand.

Broken Record

In early 2019, Unipec said it expected to trade up to 300,000 barrels per day (bpd) of U.S. crude oil by the end of the year. That would be about triple its trading volume in 2018. According to U.S. Census data, Unipec purchased one cargo that was scheduled for delivery at the end of April and another cargo in early May. Those two cargoes made for the first U.S. imports for the Chinese state-owned company since September 2018.[71]

"The Chinese import of U.S. crude oil has been hit hard even though there are no tariffs. This number fell to just 3 percent in the first four months of 2019," said Sand. "U.S. crude oil exports to China could be an important part of any trade deal the countries reach, given President Trump's focus on improving the trade balance between the two nations."

U.S. Exports to China of Crude Oil and Petroleum Products

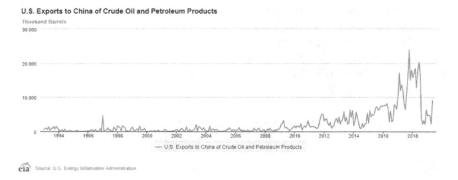

— U.S. Exports to China of Crude Oil and Petroleum Products

eia Source: U.S. Energy Information Administration

According to the EIA, the U.S. crude oil purchases from China continued into May, climbing to a nine-month high of 247,000 bpd.

With the trade war escalating again following the August 2019 announcement of additional tariffs, China being labeled a currency manipulator, and the U.S.

---

71   Ocean Zhou, "China's Unipec Resumes Crude Imports From US After 6-month Absence," S&P Global Platts, April 24, 2019

government no longer working with Huawei, the price of oil has taken a series of hits.

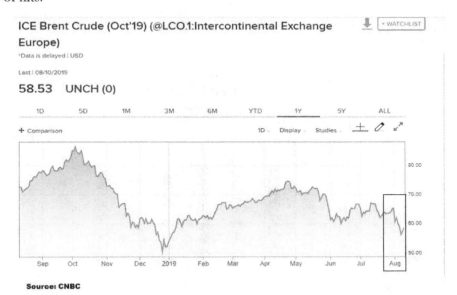

Source: CNBC

U.S. traders have also voiced their concern that this latest round of tensions could cause another China crude pullback. "I think it is a virtual shoo-in that volumes will slow to a trickle and may even grind to a complete halt," Stephen Brennock, oil analyst at PVM Oil Associates, told CNBC via email. [72]

Less than a week after China announced it was putting oil on its September retaliatory list, the June crude oil data was released. For the first time in 11 months, China was back buying U.S. oil. China purchased over 1 million tons, lifting the total seaborne U.S. crude oil exports to a record high of 11.9 million tons.[73] The trade pipe that was briefly flowing will now be shut off.

Following the LNG Trade

The first round of retaliatory tariffs did not include LNG. There was an assumption in the energy community that China would not add LNG to the list because of its appetite for consumption. That thinking was wrong.

[72] Sam Meredith, "U.S. Oil Is Likely to be China's Next Target as Trade War Rages, Energy Analysts Warn," CNBC.com, August 9, 2019

[73] Peter Sand, "Record High Seaborne US Crude Oil Exports in June 2017," BIMCO, August 27, 2019

The tensions heated up over the summer of 2018, and the United States slapped China with another tariff on $200 billion of Chinese goods. China smacked back with the unanticipated 10 percent tariffs on imports of U.S. LNG in September 2018. Prices dipped slightly.

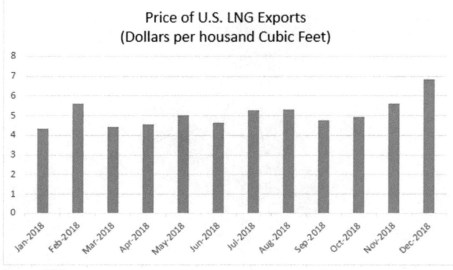

**Price of U.S. LNG Exports
(Dollars per housand Cubic Feet)**

Source: EIA

While prices stayed relatively stable, the shift in the flow of trade for U.S. LNG to China changed. Before the tariffs took effect in 2018, U.S. LNG accounted for 7 percent of China's total LNG imports from January through June. After China imposed the 10 percent tariff, from October through May 2019, U.S. LNG accounted for only 1 percent of Chinese LNG imports.

"Looking from January through May of 2019, we're back down to about .1 bcf [billion cubic feet] a day, so a drop of roughly 80 percent from the same period a year earlier, which shows the whirlwind trend of LNG," said Book. "The stark deviation from the trend only speaks to the challenge as we move forward with no resolution."

As with the transport of crude, LNG takes between one and one and a half months to travel from the United States to China. If you take the travel time into consideration, China's decision not to purchase U.S. LNG was made after President Trump's February 24, 2019, announcement that he was extending the March 1 deadline for the tariffs on $200 billion of Chinese goods, leaving them at 10 percent on an open-ended basis, and before his May 5, 2019, tweet

94

announcing that he intended to raise the tariff rate from the 10 percent originally threatened to 25 percent on May 10.

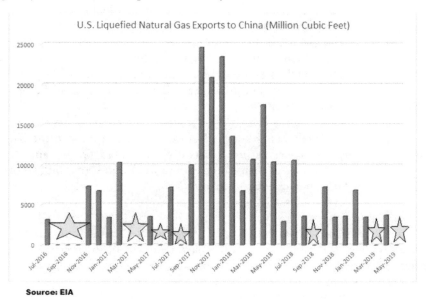

U.S. Liquefied Natural Gas Exports to China (Million Cubic Feet)

Source: EIA

On May 13, 2019, China announced it was going to increase the tariff on U.S. LNG to 25 percent, effective June 1.

Donald J. Trump ✓
@realDonaldTrump

For 10 months, China has been paying Tariffs to the USA of 25% on 50 Billion Dollars of High Tech, and 10% on 200 Billion Dollars of other goods. These payments are partially responsible for our great economic results. The 10% will go up to 25% on Friday. 325 Billions Dollars....

12:08 PM · May 5, 2019 · Twitter for iPhone

25.5K Retweets   **101.1K** Likes

Donald J. Trump ✓ @realDonaldTrump · May 5
Replying to @realDonaldTrump
....of additional goods sent to us by China remain untaxed, but will be shortly, at a rate of 25%. The Tariffs paid to the USA have had little impact on product cost, mostly borne by China. The Trade Deal with China continues, but too slowly, as they attempt to renegotiate. No!

8.2K   17.7K   75.5K

"Structurally, our trade goals are not fully compatible with China," explained Book. "What we're asking for is for them to either give up their advantage in global trade, which they're unwilling to do, or for multinationals to get out of China, and it looks like plan B is the one we're going with. So that doesn't mean the trade war is going to end. It could mean that we are going to be entering a long period of friction. And China is going to continue to do what they must do to survive. China's growth is entirely dependent on finding a higher position in the value chain in the future, and that means that they're going to be open for business with the world."

With the U.S. effectively being knocked out of the China market, the battle to dominate China's business is now between Australia, Qatar, and Russia. Australia has been China's largest source of imported LNG. In April, shipments to China surged 61.3 percent year-over-year.[74]

"China wants our gas. They want everybody's gas. You know what energy security is in China? It's as much energy as possible," said Book. "If they can find alternative, domestic resources that take them off of the reliance they have on imported hydrocarbons, they're going to do it." China has also invested in LNG projects and pipelines in the Indo-Pacific and Eurasia regions. "It's all about having stable and reliable energy sources with easier access," explained Book. "These deals also take away potential Chinese investment dollars for future U.S. deals."

The knocking out of U.S. LNG exports to China has also created more opportunities for U.S. LNG competitors like Russia. Since the start of the trade war, China and Russia are working together on several LNG projects. The Power of Siberia pipeline, which is a project between China National Petroleum Corporation and Russia's Gazprom, is progressing. China has also actively invested in Russia's LNG projects, such as Yamal LNG and Arctic LNG 2. With this robust energy cooperation, the two will be able to enhance mutual interest to counter U.S. LNG production.

Other Russian LNG announcements in 2019 will add to and enhance the plumbing of LNG delivery in Asia. In January, a preliminary deal was struck between Novatek, Russia's largest LNG company, and Japan's Saibu Gas Co. The deal that would allow Novatek to store its Arctic LNG on Japan's southern island of Kyushu, as well as the possibility of building two additional LNG tanks and revamping its re-exporting ability. That would offer Russia more

---

[74]   Cindy Liang, "China's April LNG Supply From Australia Hits Record High, up 61.3% on Year," S&P Global Platts, May 27, 2019

opportunity and flexibility to meet both South Korean and Chinese demand, as well as cut costs.

Then, at the June 2019 G-20 summit in Osaka, the Japanese corporation Mitsui and the Japanese Oil, Gas and Metals National Corporation (JOGMEC, formerly known as the Japan National Oil Corporation) announced that they will participate in the second Arctic project of Novatek. Japanese Prime Minister Shinzo Abe praised the agreement and stressed that the deal "facilitates Russia's efforts to develop the Arctic and ensures stable energy supply to our country."[75]

South Korea is already in talks with Russia about the potential gas pipeline via North Korea.

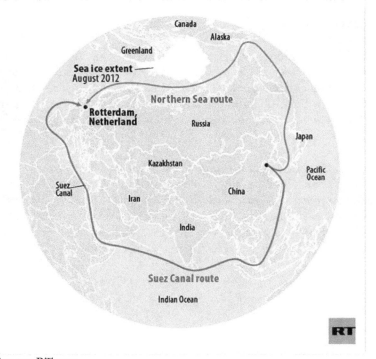

Source: RT.com

For companies like Cheniere, Tellurian, and other LNG developers that have built relationships with the Chinese state-backed companies, the 25 percent

---

[75] Press statements following talks with Prime Minister of Japan Shinzo Abe, June 29, 2019

tariff has been a blow. The much anticipated $18 billion, 20-year deal between Cheniere and China was officially put on hold per executives in a news interview that cited the uncertainty of the trade war as the reason.[76]

While the "pipes" of LNG trade are expanding for the U.S. in Europe, the blockage to China is significant to the growth of the overall U.S. LNG industry. "The problem is what we can't see—the investment decisions that aren't being made now because of uncertainty," Book stressed. "Industrial capacity has a long backlog, so this is an intermediate-horizon risk. It's likely to be visible one to two years from now, perhaps when we are looking for a swift recovery from a recession. And there's no easy way to measure it, except that the demand we're looking for might not be there. So instead of a V-shaped recovery, which is what we would want, we could be in for an L or a square root."

U.S. LNG Opportunities

Even before the trade war started, the United States was active in getting a foothold in Europe. Because of the shorter distance to Europe and the lower European pricing benchmarks of U.S. LNG, Europe is an area of growth opportunity for the United States. Energy Secretary Rick Perry has traveled to Europe many times to expand energy relations. In January 2018, U.S. European LNG exports surpassed Asian destinations.

"The question of how much energy we can put into a growing world is always going to be constrained by how fast that world is growing," Book said. "If we have an economic slowdown because of trade war, U.S. energy exports are likely to suffer across the board, and it's not going to matter whether tariffs are in place. The big issue is going to be that global consumption growth is likely to fall. GDP and oil and gas demand are pretty closely linked."

---

[76] Anjli Raval, Emiko Terazono, "U.S.-China Trade War Casts Chill Over Liquefied Natural Gas Market," Financial Times, March 29, 2019

CHAPTER FIVE

Ports and the Front-Loading Wave

Once American companies knew the tariffs would be imposed on July 6, 2018, it was a race to import their products in ahead of the deadline to avoid paying the tariff. The mass reaction created a tsunami of imports arriving at the U.S. ports. To put this surge of imports into perspective, in 2017, when it was business as usual at all U.S. ports, a total of 10,423,523 TEU (twenty-foot equivalent unit) of Chinese imports were processed.[77] In 2018, a total of 11,324,026 TEU were imported.[78] That's an increase of 900,503 containers.

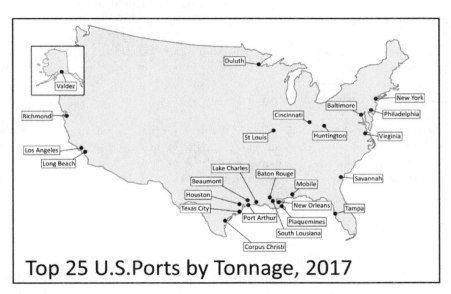

Top 25 U.S.Ports by Tonnage, 2017

Source: Marine Money International

A year and one month into the trade war, the half-year trade numbers were crunched. In August 2019, the total trade with China at all U.S. ports in the first six months of 2019 was down by 8.72 percent compared to 2018 at the same time. These results were the exact opposite of the Trump trade doctrine's goal of shrinking the trade deficit. The deficit soared.

---

77   PIERS, IHS Markit
78   PIERS, IHS Markit

Quarterly Total Trade with China (in TEU)					
	Half Year				
	2017	2018	2019	% Change 2017–2018	% Change 2018–2019
US Total	6,382,929	6,363,267	5,808,082	-0.31%	-8.72%

Source: Port of Los Angeles, PIERS, IHS Markit

Unlike commodities and agricultural products, which require a transaction before they are transported, companies that manufacture overseas strike their own deals with retailers; their products can be transported to a warehouse and moved when needed.

Container shipping is also faster than commodity transport. Importers can use an express service vessel, for which travel time is approximately 12 to 14 days on sea. These vessels shave 4 to 6 days off the normal travel by skipping ports.[79] They also come with a higher price tag.

The business of the ports has a cycle that is centered around the buying habits of the consumer. The first peak season runs from around June to September of every year, for back-to-school shopping; the next occurs from October through December, during the major Western holidays and leading up to Chinese New Year.

Retail Tariff Reaction

The retail industry was not surprised when President Trump initiated the use of tariffs. During the transition of then President Elect Trump, the National Retail Federation (NRF) organized a meeting of its policy council (made up of government relations heads from the retail companies and NRF members) with a Trump transition team member to talk about the administration's economic agenda.

The group met at the Capitol Hill Club. "Everett Eissenstat,[80] who at the time was the chief international trade counsel for the Senate Finance Trade

---

[79] Ocean Audit

[80] Everett Eissenstat also served as deputy director of the National Economic Council and deputy assistant to President Trump for international economic affairs from June 8, 2017 to July 2018

Committee, was working on the transition with the administration. One of the topics in this briefing was the upcoming trade agenda," said David French, senior vice president of government relations at the National Retail Federation. "The most sobering thing he said at that meeting was that the president had virtually *unlimited* authority to impose tariffs and other trade barriers. He brought along with him a Congressional Resource book, which detailed all the various authorities that the president had lateral control of. So we were aware of the president's intentions on tariffs and started contemplating the issues immediately."

Chinese factories are an essential part of the U.S. retail supply chain. Lower production costs enable them to considerably mark up their products. Walmart imports 26 percent of its merchandise from China; Target, 34 percent; Dick Sporting Goods, 51 percent; and Bed Bath and Beyond, 53 percent.[81] For tech giant Apple, you will find their products stamped, "Designed by Apple in California, assembled in China." When the United States imposed a tariff of 25 percent on 818 categories of goods imported from China in the first round of tariffs, the price tag of these products was $50 billion.

The Port of Los Angeles is the largest container port in the United States, and China is its number one customer. The total cargo value generated by this trade before the start of the trade war was $153 billion. The port's second largest trade partner, Japan, was valued at $36 billion in cargo. This dramatic difference shows how important business with China is for the Port of Los Angeles. Gene Seroka, executive director of the Port of Los Angeles, said 55 percent of cargo that comes into the port has a tariff or tax on it, and 98 percent of Chinese goods have tariffs. "It takes *seven* Vietnams to make a China," he said. "What we said in 2018 still holds true, that there would be consumer impacts. Prices in certain sectors have gone up."

Furniture is the number one commodity imported from China, followed by apparel, plastic products, and footwear. Out of the top 10 categories, based on the container count, apparel and automobile parts led the surge in front-loading. The rush of containers with goods subject to the tariff started to arrive in late spring.

---

[81] Michael Lasser, "U.S. Hardline and Grocery Retail How Will Tariffs Factor Into Retail Reporting Season?" UBS, May 13, 2019

POLA Containerized Import from China (Calendar Year)

Rank	Commodity	2017	2018	Difference	% Change
1	FURNITURE	390,610	405,779	15,168	3.9%
2	APPAREL	133,090	158,379	25,289	19.0%
3	PLASTIC PRODS, MISC	146,324	157,489	11,165	7.6%
4	FOOTWARE	131,775	144,722	12,947	9.8%
5	ELECTRONIC PRODUCTS	138,398	143,138	4,740	3.4%
6	TOYS	148,130	138,371	-9,759	-6.6%
7	GENERAL CARGO, MISC	124,605	124,566	-39	0.0%
8	AUTOMOBILE PARTS	99,183	121,845	22,662	22.8%
9	LAMPS & PARTS	85,001	89,746	4,745	5.6%
10	HOUSEHOLD APPLIANCES	81,970	89,379	7,409	9.0%

Source: Port of Los Angeles PIERS, IHS Markit

The July 1 tariffs were the fourth official round of tariffs imposed by the United States and the largest in terms of volume. The containers loaded with solar panels and washing machines that had been front-loaded for each of their own tariffs were a small fraction compared to what the ports soon started receiving.

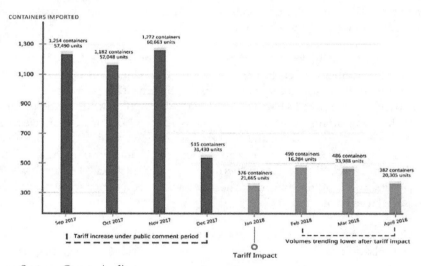

Source: Ocean Audit

Preparing for the Wave

It is the mission of the nation's ports to move incoming and outgoing containers, cargo, and fuel as efficiently as possible. A new communication system at the Port of Los Angeles was designed to give port management an advanced look at the volume of loads coming from Asia. This information provided a deeper line of sight into the number of arriving containers so the port could be better prepared.

"Traditionally we would get pieces of information and a full view of the vessels just two days before they got to the port," explained Seroka. "Now we were seeing this information 14, 21, and as many as 38 days before a vessel came to L.A. We not only had the data of where the cargo was going, we would also have an idea in the way it would travel out of our port once it was unloaded, by truck or rail."

The data tracking offered Seroka and his leadership team key insight into the tremendous volumes heading their way. They held numerous meetings with their customers and shipping lines to create an action plan for the container surge. With the volume of imports expected to more than double, the port would need to have more workers to move the containers. "The industry signed up an additional 1,000 registered longshore persons and 5,000 casuals," Seroka said. "Casuals are akin to apprentices. So an approximate total of 12,000 longshore folks were readied. For the first time in a generation, we saw an influx of an additional 6,000 workers, 1,000 that were ready to go on the job day one."

On an average day before the trade war began, the Port of Los Angeles processed 10 vessels; the Port of Long Beach processed eight. "For argument's sake, the front-loading increased that number of vessels to 14 and 10," said Seroka. "We also worked through the largest exchange value ever. Each ship got bigger. We were doing more boxes on and off. The average time those ships were in port depended on their size, and they were there anywhere between three and five days." A normal stay for a vessel before the trade war was two to three days.

The container volume was so big at the port that additional operators were also assembled at the railroad truckers' terminals to move the containers as quickly as possible. The intricate network of plumbing to unload the containers off the vessels and onto trucks or rails needed to be continuous. Time is money. If a container sits for any reason it literally clogs the logistical system. All pieces of the supply chain need to move—including the trucks.

"There was so much cargo coming in," Seroka continued. "Although we did a good job working on the water side, you started to see longer dwell times at the terminal because of the longer truck wait times, and then longer street dwell times because those containers were on chassis not being moved. Truck chassis became mini-warehouses."

Containers were stored on truck chassis because there was a lack of space at area warehouses as a result of the dramatic increase of containers. The storage challenge has persisted into the second half of 2019. In a report by commercial real estate services firm Cushman & Wakefield, the vacancy rate for the Los Angeles market was 1.7 percent for the second quarter of 2019. The nationwide vacancy rates of warehouses were between 4 to 5 percent. The historic vacancy average for the greater L.A. area was 3.1 percent.

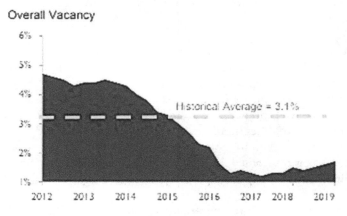

Source: Cushman & Wakefield

"Using truck chassis was essentially an inventory play," Seroka said. "Trucks are a vital part of the intermodal system to move product out of the port. Less available truck chassis meant you had to wait longer to move out the containers."

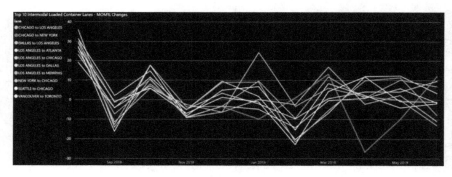

Trade War

Hours before the United States officially imposed the July 6, 2018, tariffs on China, China accused the United States of instigating a trade war.

"We don't want a trade war but have to fight if it is necessary for upholding the interest of the country and people," said Gao Feng, spokesman for China's

Ministry of Commerce, at a press conference. "China will absolutely not fire the first shot. However, we have no choice but to strike back if the U.S. imposes tariffs. What the U.S. is doing is total backpedaling. We believe that people in the world understand and support China, just as the Chinese saying goes, 'A just cause enjoys abundant support while an unjust cause finds little support.' We call on all countries to take collective actions in order to firmly oppose trade protectionism and unilateralism and protect the common interest of all people in the world."[82]

In retaliation, China imposed a 25 percent tariff on 545 U.S. goods (worth $34 billion), which smacked down U.S. exports to China.

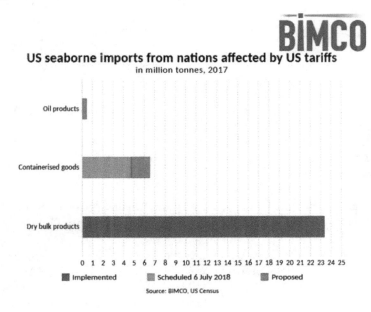

US seaborne imports from nations affected by US tariffs
in million tonnes, 2017

Source: BIMCO, US Census

Instead of narrowing the trade imbalance between China and the United States, the trade war exacerbated the trade deficit. U.S. exports to China dropped like a stone in June 2018, a full month before the tariffs hit. From October through December, U.S. exports were at their lowest levels, reaching -35 percent.

At the onset of the tariffs, U.S. exporters told Seroka they were getting squeezed. "Our exporting companies saw volume just drop off," Seroka explained. "We saw rises in volume ahead of the tariff implementation dates,

---

[82] Regular Press Conference of the Ministry of Commerce (July 5, 2018), July 6, 2018, 10:53 BJT, MOFCOM

and then on the export side we were down every single month in calendar year 2018," he continued. "Our best month was down 9 percent. Our worst month was at the end of the year, and that was down 45 percent year-over-year."

Figure 1: U.S. Exports, Imports, and the Trade Deficit with China, January 2018–May 2019

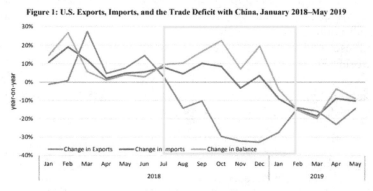

Source: U.S. Census Bureau, Trade in Goods with China, July 3, 2019. *https://www.census.gov/foreign-trade/balance/c5700.html.*

The biggest casualty of the trade war has been U.S. scrap metal. On August 23, 2018, China, the largest consumer of scrap commodities, imposed retaliatory tariffs on U.S. aluminum waste and scrap. U.S. scrap metal exports out of the Port of Los Angeles were down 67 percent in 2018. Waste and paper products were down 22 percent.

"These folks got hit twice, between the environmental policies and tariffs," said Seroka. "Wastepaper was the largest export out of our country."

The impact of China's decrease in agriculture purchases was also clearly seen and felt at the ports. Soybean exports out of the Port of Los Angeles were down 61 percent in 2018, and meat, both fresh and frozen, was down 16 percent. Other export categories in the red were hides, skins, and furs, down 25 percent; plastic products, down 22 percent; and pet and animal feeds, down 22 percent.

The trade war escalated throughout the summer of 2018 and continued into the fall, at which point the second round of tariffs were increased to a list of $200 billion worth of Chinese imports. One of those items was flooring. Initially the tariff amount was set at 10 percent and would begin on September 24, 2018. Then, starting January 1, 2019, that tariff amount would increase to 25 percent. The pressure was on for flooring manufacturers and retailers to get their product in.

The flow of trade can be monitored by the bills of lading. Vinyl tile, for example, was shown by bills of lading to be one of the products subjected to tariff in the second round.

POLA Containerized Export to China (Calendar Year)

Rank	Commodity	2017	2018	Difference	% Change
1	PAPER & PAPERBOARD, INCL WASTE	183,050	143,782	-39,267	-21.5%
2	PET& ANIMAL FEEDS	31,198	24,471	-6,727	-21.6%
3	FABRICS, INCL RAW COTTON	21,325	22,794	1,470	6.9%
4	GENERAL CARGO, MISC	17,887	19,498	1,611	9.0%
5	AUTOMOBILE PARTS	15,922	15,630	-292	-1.8%
6	RESINS	17,857	15,510	-2,347	-13.1%
7	SCRAP METAL	43,997	14,464	-29,532	-67.1%
8	LOGS & LUMBER	12,728	9,522	-3,206	-25.2%
9	BORIC ACID, HYDROCHLORIC ACID	4,903	9,310	4,407	89.9%
10	RUGS & FLOOR COVERINGS	6,924	7,027	104	1.5%
11	HIDES, SKINS, FURS	9,176	6,874	-2,303	-25.1%
12	UNCLASSIFIABLE CHEMICALS	3,441	6,528	3,087	89.7%
13	EMPTY CONTAINERS, DRUMS ETC	1,772	6,277	4,506	254.3%
14	WOOD PULP	2,395	5,837	3,442	143.7%
15	ELECTRONIC PRODUCTS	4,753	4,806	53	1.1%
16	SOYBEANS & PRODS	11,206	4,399	-6,807	-60.7%
17	SOD CMP, ARSENATE-BORATE	3,900	3,962	63	1.6%
18	PLASTIC PRODS, MISC	4,639	3,620	-1,019	-22.0%
19	NEWSPAPERS	3,543	3,467	-75	-2.1%
20	MEAT, CHIEFLY FRESH&FROZEN	4,011	3,357	-654	-16.3%

Source: Port of Los Angeles, PIERS, IHS Markit

"In July and August of 2018, before the tariff was implied and hearings began, there 318 million pounds of vinyl tiles were imported," explained Steve Ferreira, CEO of Ocean Audit. "The volumes then changed, and you saw the front-loading surge during the time period of the 10 percent tariff. The difference in pounds was huge. Retailers like Home Depot were racing to get their product in before the tariffs increased."

To offset the 10 percent increase, U.S. flooring companies like Armstrong Flooring announced they were raising prices. Just days before the tariff was imposed, Don Maier, president and CEO of Armstrong at that time, said they would increase prices on luxury vinyl tile, engineered wood flooring, and rigid core flooring, starting October 1. He also added that they would implement another price increase effective January 1 to offset the 25 percent tariff. Maier said the increased prices were "unavoidable" due to the tariff.[83]

---

[83]   "Armstrong Announces Chinese Tariff-Related Price Increase," Floor Daily, September 20, 2018

"The trickle down of the price increase can be seen at the store level," said Ferreira. "The consumer was paying double to offset that 10 percent tariff."

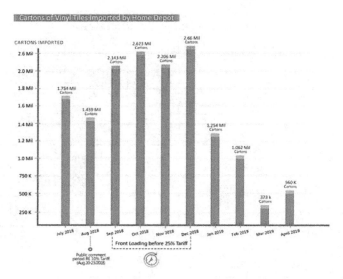

Another household item on the $200 billion list was mattresses. While many big brands are made in the United States, like Tempur Sealy, China was a large supplier. According to Panjiva, $1 billion worth of mattresses were imported during a 12-month window that ended May 31, 2018. Out of that billion-dollar segment, $850 million worth was imported from China.

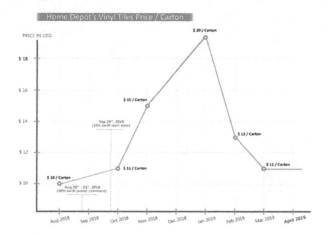

Amazon's mattresses are manufactured in China. Based on the flow of the company's containers, we know the front-loading began in September, just ahead of the tariff being implemented, but increased in earnest ahead of the threat of the tariff increasing from 10 percent to 25 percent.

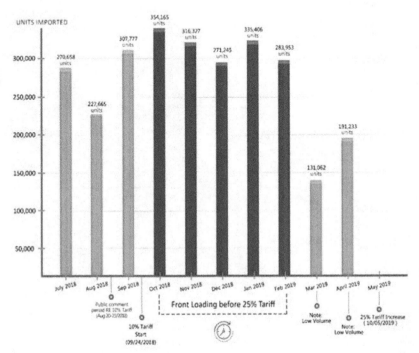

Units of mattresses Imported by Amazon

Source: Ocean Audit

"A shipment is essentially a blueprint between a buyer, an importer, and a producer and exporter," explained Ferreira. "There is a buying process that goes behind this. First there is negotiation on how many pieces will be manufactured and at what price point. Then the company and manufacturer would agree on the frequency of the orders to ensure a proper supply chain into the warehouses. The threat of tariffs hangs over this planning process."

Ocean Audit performed a study on the pricing of Amazon's mattresses to see if there was any impact on the consumer. "The average retail price on Amazon's mattresses were stable until the front-loading began," Ferreira said. "That was when we saw a price increase. This was before the tariff began."

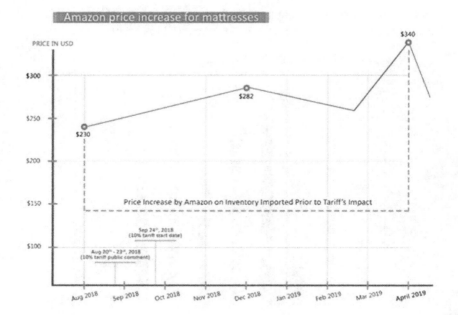

Source: Ocean Audit

Fourth-Quarter Surge

The high volumes of Chinese imports flowed into the fourth quarter with the threat of the tariff on the $200 billion of Chinese goods increasing to 25 percent. The volumes were tremendous. Mario Cordero, executive director of the Port of Long Beach, the third largest container port in the United States, said, "If you compare the 2018 fourth quarter to the 2017 fourth quarter, the surge was essentially 33 percent."

In a typical December, the port services approximately 180 vessels. In December of 2018, Cordero said 31 additional vessels were unloaded. The extra capacity started to slow the flow of trade at the port. Ordinarily, after a vessel enters the port, the containers are unloaded and stored. Trucks then line up to pick up a container and have it loaded onto their chassis to be transported.

Example of Container Terminal Cargo Loading and Unloading

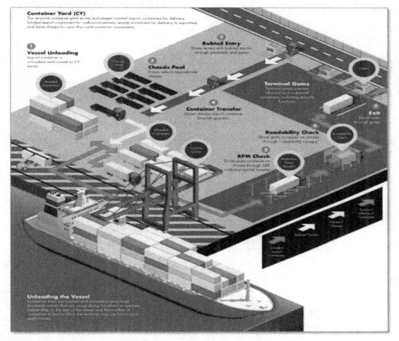

Source: U.S. Department of Transportation, Bureau of Transportation Statistics, Port Performance Freight Statistics Annual Report to Congress 2018 (Washington, DC: 2018). https://doi.org/10.21949/1502601

"That didn't happen," explained Cordero. "With the front-loading of cargo, it created a disruption in terms of the number of empty containers we had at the port with nowhere to go, so those empty containers were either on a chassis, at a warehouse, or at particular terminals because there was nowhere to move them."

The problem of space was exacerbated by this growing number of empty containers. In 2017, before the trade war started, 39 percent of Long Beach's exports went to China. In 2018, that number dropped to around 27 percent. "Anytime you have a disruption at the level that we've had, it's going to be difficult for the American exporter to all of a sudden identify new markets to replace the common market they've had with Asia, more specifically China," Cordero said. "The demand for Chinese imports by the American consumer has remained steady. However, our exports to China have certainly suffered."

Cordero explained that the void of China exports his clients faced could not be filled. "In the first six months of 2019, our overall exports were 11.7 percent. That's *all* countries. So other countries were not picking up the slack."

China is a large bucket to fill. It is also number one trading partner with the Port of Long Beach. Seventy percent of the goods that pass through the port either originate from China or are transported there.

The drop in U.S. exports was the biggest indicator of the lack of progression in the trade talks. There was no way around it, and no amount of rhetoric could alter the facts. The impact of China's lack of buying was felt across the nation. U.S. exports to China were down 24.54 percent in 2018.

Trade with China (Calendar Year)									
	Imports			Exports			Total		
	2017	2018	% Change	2017	2018	% Change	2017	2018	% Change
US Total	10,374,099	11,326,347	9.18%	2,781,486	2,099,275	-24.53%	13,155,585	13,425,622	2.05%
West Coast	6,640,869	7,158,921	7.80%	1,439,720	1,093,354	-24.06%	8,080,589	8,252,275	2.12%
San Pedro Bay	5,367,677	5,766,000	7.42%	979,887	764,472	-21.98%	6,347,564	6,530,472	2.88%
Los Angeles	2,759,772	3,010,804	9.10%	500,137	410,463	-17.93%	3,259,909	3,421,267	4.95%
Long Beach	2,607,905	2,755,196	5.65%	479,750	354,009	-26.21%	3,087,655	3,109,205	0.70%

Source: Port of Los Angeles, PIERS, IHS Markit

Long-Term Impact

Seroka emphasized that this tariff-based lockout was not just about the present. The trade war would have long-lasting implications. "Soybeans, hay, wheat, beans really got dinged," said Seroka. "What we are finding is that China was sourcing from other countries to replace our products. So if a trade deal does get done, you have to understand we can't flip a switch and China starts buying from the U.S. again. These relationships China have created with other countries to replace U.S. goods are multiyear relationships and are forward-looking." The imbalance of the containers flowing in and out of the ports was striking. While exports continued to decline from the Port of Los Angeles, import volumes increased so much that additional vessels were added into the rotation.

The heavy volumes quickly filled up container storage at the ports and warehouses. For example, if a terminal has 100 acres available for container storage and they fill 80 acres, it is considered "full capacity" because you need the roadways and pathways to be available for trucks to move and pick up or drop off their containers. With the acres on the ground filled, the only way to store the containers was to go was up. Through agreements between employers and labor unions at the Port of Los Angeles, the maximum container stack is six high. "We don't want to do anything beyond that, for health and safety purposes," explained Seroka. "Also, when you start stacking six high and have a tarmac completely full of containers, you have to phantom moves to get to the box that trucker wants. Sometimes we had containers a truck driver needed to transport that was literally at the bottom of a pile. We would need to move six containers in order to retrieve it."

The fear of getting smacked with tariffs had importers changing the destinations of their containers to other ports that might not be as congested. They needed to make sure their containers would get in before the tariff was imposed. This strategy caused a dichotomy of pain and opportunity for the ports.

PORT SHARE — Q2 2019 VS 2016-18 AVERAGE

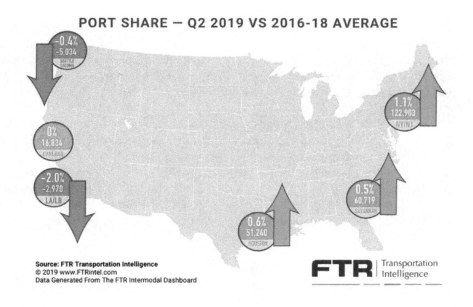

Source: FTR Transportation Intelligence
© 2019 www.FTRintel.com
Data Generated From The FTR Intermodal Dashboard

FTR | Transportation Intelligence

"It is important to remember when a container is diverted it is not a one-off," stressed Seroka. "These are not transactional deals. Typically, port changes can start off as seasonal, and move to annual and then multiyear agreements. So once folks decide to leave and go with somebody else, they're going to be locked in for a while. That is by design, because you want to build surety in your supply chain."

Part of that port supply chain that provided challenges was the increasing volume of empty containers. The lack of U.S. exports to China created a glut of empty containers. This was a problem because an empty container does not travel on a vessel for free. Seroka said costs are either absorbed by the shipping line or passed along in import/export costs. Because of the massive number of empty containers, the environment was rough and left little room for negotiation. Shipping line companies were forced to absorb the costs. In August 2019, the price to transport an empty container on the transpacific trade route was approximately $250.[84]

Rising to the Challenge

Based on their location, it makes sense that the ports in the United States all handle a variety of U.S. exports. For example, the Port of Oakland is considered America's agricultural gateway. The port's major exports are all food related: grain, fruits, wine and other alcoholic beverages, meat, pork, and poultry. They also export paper and plastic.

Chris Lytle, who retired as executive director of the Port of Oakland in June 2019, said that the volume between exports and imports at the port were typically 55-45. This differentiated the Port of Oakland from the ports of L.A. and Long Beach, which are more reliant on imports.

"Even though it is not by a huge margin, we are primarily an export market," explained Lytle. "We were very concerned about Trump's trade policies because when you start manipulating free trade and put in all kinds of new restrictions and rules, it throws that market equilibrium totally out of whack. We saw the import numbers pick up, which we were very happy about, but on the export side, like most ports servicing China, we saw a significant drop-off. Our exporters needed to expand into existing or new markets to offset the loss of China trade."

The agriculture industry in the Oakland area went into overdrive in its pursuit of new markets. July 2019 was the Port of Oakland's busiest month in its 92-year history. For the first time, Oakland's import volume was more than the 90,000-container threshold in a single month. U.S. exports also jumped 10.2 percent in July 2019 compared to July 2018.

The fifth-straight month of year-over-year gains in export volume was *not* due to surging U.S. exports to China. The gains in exports were a result of increased exports to Vietnam, South Korea, Japan, and Taiwan. "Our expanding exports

---

[84] Port of Los Angeles, August 2019

during this trade war showed the ingenuity of our customers," said Lytle. "They were finding new markets."

For the first half of 2019, total exports out of the Port of Oakland increased by 2.4 percent. The big 2019 exports out of the port included almonds, meat, oranges, and hay. The Port of Oakland's exports to China outpaced the national average of U.S. exports to the world, which was 1.58 percent.

First Half Year US Containerized Volume (in TEU)

	2018	2019	% Change of 2018 to 2019
Exports	6,450,169	6,551,922	1.58%
Imports	11,308,277	11,666,466	3.17%
Grand Total	17,758,447	18,218,388	2.59%

Source: Port of Los Angeles, PIERS, IHS Markit

In June, Seroka wrote a letter to the USTR voicing his concerns of a new round of tariffs being imposed on the $300 billion of Chinese products. Seroka said that based on the Port of Los Angeles's analysis, the additional tariffs would be passed on to consumers and the front-loading would impact port operations.

In the first half of 2019, the Port of Los Angeles saw a decrease in trade with China by 0.03 percent compared to the same time period in 2018. Nationwide, trade was down 8.72 percent in the first six months year-over-year.

Quarterly Total Trade with China (in TEU)

	1Q					2Q					Half Year				
	2017	2018	2019	% Change 2017-2018	% Change 2018-2019	2017	2018	2019	% Change 2017-2018	% Change 2018-2019	2017	2018	2019	% Change 2017-2018	% Change 2018-2019
US Total	3,075,318	3,179,354	2,798,237	3.38%	-11.99%	3,307,611	3,183,913	3,009,845	-3.74%	-5.47%	6,382,929	6,363,267	5,808,082	-0.31%	-8.72%
West Coast	1,840,319	1,882,429	1,611,827	2.29%	-13.31%	2,072,612	1,995,002	1,829,401	-3.74%	-8.30%	3,912,931	3,877,421	3,461,229	-0.91%	-10.73%
San Pedro Bay	1,422,099	1,496,124	1,271,832	5.21%	-15.00%	1,624,819	1,583,119	1,458,725	-2.57%	-7.86%	3,046,918	3,079,243	2,730,367	1.06%	-11.33%
Los Angeles	779,324	734,556	702,353	-5.74%	-4.38%	808,164	791,508	823,259	-2.06%	4.01%	1,587,488	1,526,064	1,525,610	-3.87%	-0.03%
Long Beach	642,775	761,568	569,281	18.48%	-25.25%	816,655	791,610	635,476	-3.07%	-19.72%	1,459,430	1,553,179	1,204,757	6.42%	-22.43%

Source: Port of Los Angeles, PIERS, IHS Markit

"Imports with China are down 10 percent, but we are making it up in other locations like South Korea and Japan. But for every shipping container the port gains from other countries, it loses two and a half from what it got from China," said Seroka. "We don't see a way out of this until [the U.S. and China] come to an active negotiated settlement. Bottom line: The shipments would need to increase significantly between more than just a few countries to keep the port on par with its numbers."

The Tariff Squeeze

Navigating the tariffs added a level of uncertainty for companies trying to plan. Many U.S. companies like Casabella, a part of Bradshaw Home, innovate their product design in the United States but manufacture the majority of their products in China. Because Casabella sells household and cleaning products, it always has products being transported by sea.

Before the trade war, it would normally take 90 to 120 days from the time Casabella ordered its products for the containers to arrive in the U.S. (60 to 90 days of production, then 30 days on the water). "We have goods on the water right now that were ordered four to five months ago," said Bruce Kaminstein, founder of Casabella. "We have products coming in where the prices with retailers were pre-negotiated. Now they are going to be 15 percent more expensive. We must go back to retailers now and renegotiate a price increase to help offset the 15 percent tariff. The trade war has put us in the middle of a squeeze play with the retailers."

Kaminstein explained the tug of war between the retailers and companies like Casabella: "The retailers want to hold their pricing because they know if they raise prices, they will sell less product. So, if the retailers don't agree to raise prices, the added costs must be offset somewhere—that means our bottom line, which impacts company expansion and jobs. That is not good for America."

Kaminstein said he began fierce discussions to see if Casabella's Chinese manufacturers could drop the price of manufacturing their products. "Unfortunately, I know they will not drop the price by 10 to 15 percent."

While the company's buckets and large plastic products are made in the U.S., their houseware products that require certain materials, such as bristles, or manual labor are made in China—and moving those operations to the United States is not possible. "It is essentially impossible to make these products in America," Kaminstein declared. "There is no place to bristle a broom! There used to be original equipment manufacturers (OEMs) in the U.S., but they are all gone now. We use the world to produce our innovations now."

On Earth Day, April 22, 2020, Casabella will officially roll out a new product line, but because of the September tariffs, the sales team must revert and create a new sales plan to offset the tariff. The cost of the new product line and how much the company negotiated with retailers to sell the products for were set in July 2019. Now the product will be at least 15 percent more. Kaminstein said they must go back and renegotiate the sales price to offset the tariff. "It's very upsetting," he said.

On August 30, just two days before the next round of tariffs were set to go into effect, President Trump called the tariffs "small" and said companies that are complaining during the trade war are being mismanaged.

Donald J. Trump ✅
@realDonaldTrump

If the Fed would cut, we would have one of the biggest Stock Market increases in a long time. Badly run and weak companies are smartly blaming these small Tariffs instead of themselves for bad management...and who can really blame them for doing that? Excuses!

10:10 AM · Aug 30, 2019 · Twitter for iPhone

9.7K Retweets   **37.4K** Likes

Kaminstein said the president should not be blaming companies. "It is difficult for companies to absorb a 15 percent cost increase on short notice," he said. "Our economy for over 30 years has been global. Companies have been focusing efforts on innovation and have produced some of the best products in the world utilizing the worlds contract factories. Our global supply chain cannot be changed overnight. It is not possible to bring production to the U.S. factories that do not exist to produce branded product. We are not to be blamed in this trade war."

Kaminstein is just one of many business leaders trying to lead their companies during this chaotic time. On August 28, more than 160 business associations signed a letter addressed to President Trump urging him to delay the tariffs.

"These tariff rate increases—some starting as early as Sunday—come at the worst possible time, right in the middle of the busy holiday shipping period.... With some products facing tariffs as high as 30 percent, many businesses will have no choice but to pass along those costs to consumers. Price increases will hit shoppers just as they are making their holiday purchases.... And because these tariffs were announced with little warning, it is impossible for U.S. importers to share the burden with supply chain partners in China or shift their production to other countries. The full adverse impact of these tariff increases will be felt entirely in the United States and could represent one of the largest tax increases in American history."

The NRF was one of the trade associations that signed the letter. "If you cut the United States off from the rest of the world, globalization continues without us," warned French. "The result is you have people consuming fewer American products and Americans possibly paying more for the products they consume from abroad. It's a catastrophic miscalculation."

In the September round of tariffs, new industries, including the $148.7 billion industry of specialty foods, were targeted. "This tariff hits the small import food businesses hard," said Phil Kafarakis, president of the Specialty Food Association. "There is not a lot of wiggle room in their margins."

In addition to the margin squeeze, the impact of the front-loading at the ports and the fears of a transport slowdown were also of top concern. Many of these products are perishable, and any delay at the ports would impact their bottom line. "Specialty food warehouses usually have a three-month inventory of nonperishable products. Perishable products, on the other hand, are ordered with the foreign manufacturer at a 30-day minimum," explained Kafarakis.

The popular niche food industry was smacked with another round of tariffs, this time against the European Union. The World Trade Organization ruled in the United States' favor in imposing tariffs in its 15-year legal battle between Airbus and Boeing over subsidies.[85] The Trump administration would impose a 10 percent tariff on E.U. aircraft and a 25 percent tariff ranging on European wine, Italian parmesan, charcuterie, Scotch whisky, and clothing.

"This latest round of tariffs on the E.U. will hit the consumer just in time for the holidays," explained Kafarakis. "The president is calling this a big win for the United States. This tariff measure only escalates uncertainty for the U.S. and E.U. economies. The tit-for-tat tariffs will only continue. The Trump administration is playing a game of tariff chicken."

The tariffs are set to begin on October 18, 2019. "The tariff against the bloc begins just three days *after* the traditional start of holiday food imports," Kafarakis said. "Items will already be in transit on the water, and that means pricing for the holiday shipments have already been negotiated with retailers, and now the entire industry is being hit with 25 percent tariff on goods. How can you plan for that? You can't! It is not a cop-out. It is not what the president is now calling 'bad management.' It is the reality of the chaos these tariffs have injected into the marketplace."

The E.U. bilateral trade flow pipe has already been constricted with the 232 steel and aluminum retaliation. Retaliatory tariffs priced out over $3 billion of U.S. goods in the E.U. marketplace. One hundred and eighty types of products, including whiskey, navy beans, and motorcycles, were hit hard.

---

[85] "European Communities and Certain Member States—Measures Affecting Trade in Large Civil Aircraft," WTO ruling, October 2, 2019

This trade war has heated up with another round of tariffs. This is impacting the flow of trade between the two markets. In the first half of 2019, the deficit rose more than 9 percent (valued at $83 billion) when compared to 2018, when the tariffs and retaliatory tariffs were imposed.[86]

Trade (% of GDP)

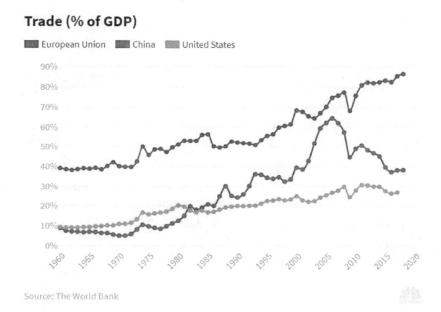

■ European Union   ■ China   ■ United States

Source: The World Bank

"Moving the supply chain to other countries is not an option," said Kafarakis. "Our community is responsible for getting new foreign suppliers vetted through government food quality and safety process. It would take six to nine months given the food safety laws within the Federal Information Security Management Act [FISMA; replaced in 2014 by the Federal Information Security Modernization Act]. It would be a real nightmare that will cost money and time."

Uncertainty Impact

Cordero said that one of the biggest miscalculations in this trade war with China was President Trump's constant telegraphing of tariff negotiations. "This on-again, off-again, and finally on-again tariff plan has not only greatly impacted

---

[86] United States Census, Trade in Goods with European Union for months of January 2019–June 2019

American business strategy and planning, it has also created a level of fear in the global markets we have never seen, because you don't know what the president will do," he explained. "He says the tariffs are on, then days later he calls them off, and then they are back on again. And through it all, there have been *no* major concessions made by the Chinese. No one wins in a trade war. The reality is U.S. importers are paying the tariffs, not the Chinese. Based on the drop in U.S. exports to China, China is not buying American goods. The U.S. is not winning."

Seroka, who is a member of the Los Angeles Area Chamber of Commerce, travels to Washington on a regular basis to speak with the Department of Commerce. "We are telling them we are seeing money on the sidelines," he said. "From companies who traditionally invest more capital into their facilities to drive more business, hire more folks, et cetera, to research and development, there is hold up."

He continued: "Normally in a boom you hear discussions and see an expansion in warehousing, trucks, clean technology, and automation. You are not hearing a lot of chatter about that now. Instead it's the empty containers, higher consumer prices, lower profitability for American companies and uncertainty in the maritime supply chain. Where is the win?"

CHAPTER SIX

Container Crunch

The front-loading and the lack of U.S. exports impacted not only the ports but also the critical transportation plumbing connecting the ports to the rest of the country. That system is called the intermodal system: the movement of freight by road, rail, and inland waterways. By tonnage and value, trucks carry the most freight in the United States, with railroads and waterways also carrying significant volumes over long distances.[87] It is also the largest single source of U.S. freight rail revenue.[88]

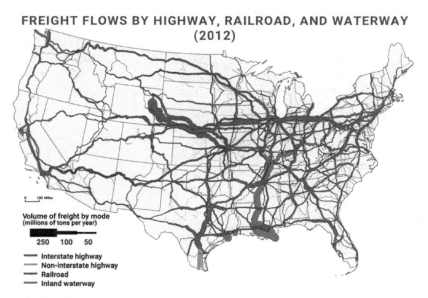

FREIGHT FLOWS BY HIGHWAY, RAILROAD, AND WATERWAY (2012)

Volume of freight by mode
(millions of tons per year)

250 100 50

— Interstate highway
— Non-interstate highway
— Railroad
— Inland waterway

SOURCE: Provided by FTR Transportation Intelligence, Highways: U.S. Department of Transportation, Federal Highway Administration, Freight Analysis Framework, Version 4.2, 2016; Rail: Federal Rail Administration, 2013 Annual Carload Waybill Sample; Inland Waterways: U.S. Army Corps of Engineers, Navigation Data Center, Waterborne Commerce Statistics Center, 2012 Waterway Network Link Commodity Data.

With so much physical supply in the system, the pipes of the intermodal network quickly narrowed. Warehouses filled up and full containers spilled over into makeshift storage solutions, which stressed the system. On the flip side,

---

87   "Freight Facts & Figures 2017, Chapter 3: The Freight Transportation System," Bureau of Transportation Statistics

88   "Rail Intermodal Keeps America Moving," Association of American Railroads, June 2018

China's infrequent buying of U.S. exports backed up empty containers to historic volumes. The intermodal system was caught in the freight undertow.

The movement of trade by containers is a 20th-century invention. In 1956, truck company owner Malcolm McLean invented and patented the standardized container. Before bulk movement with containers, the only way to transport items from vessels to those various other modes of transportation was by unloading and reloading each item *individually*. This "break bulk" cargo method was painstakingly slow and took special training for dock personnel.

As a trucker, McLean realized if you created a box for global transport that was standard in size, it could move seamlessly between various modes of transportation without the contents being unloaded. As a result, the goods would arrive at their destination faster.

During that time, McLean had the largest trucking company in the American South and the fifth largest in the nation. In his business, the more efficiently you could haul product to and from a destination, the more transport jobs you could complete. The quicker turnaround of product translated into savings for his customers. It would be a win for all.

On April 26, 1956, McLean loaded 58 trailer vans (now called containers) onto a refitted tanker ship, the SS *Ideal X*, and traveled from Port Newark, New Jersey, to the Port of Houston, Texas. It was a defining moment in maritime history. Containerization was officially born.

Swollen Container Volumes

Before the trade war, growth of domestic intermodal freight volume was forecast to be 5.5 percent for the fourth quarter of 2018. Once the tariff threats were made, importers raced to move their product into the United States before tariffs were imposed. The influx of volumes increased forecast growth rates for domestic intermodal volumes 6.9 percent from prior-year levels.[89]

Eric Starks, FTR Transportation Intelligence chairman and CEO, explained that intermodal freight is a great barometer for understanding pressures in the system because of its concentrated size.[90] "Intermodal represents 3 percent of all trade moved in the United States," he said. "By analyzing the international

---

[89] FTR Transportation Intelligence gathers and analyzes freight data from all modes of transportation and provides tracking for over 209 commodity groups.

[90] FTR Transportation Intelligence

freight coming in and the domestic freight moving versus the *traditional* seasonal behavior, it was easy to validate the front-loading early."

Frontloading
October 2017-October 2019

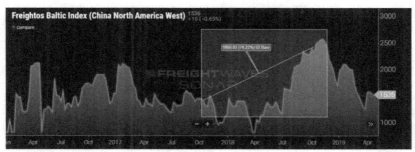

Data Source: SONAR

According to data analysis by FTR, the normal buying pattern of U.S. importers takes place in a three-month window during the second quarter of the year, when customers are preordering or premoving products into the market. Because of the travel time of containers on the water, FTR characterizes the third quarter as being the strongest quarter traditionally for intermodal transportation. However, when the front-loading started, the flow changed.

"What was radically different about the 2018 cycle was that at the start of the trade war we saw a movement of freight into the *fourth* quarter. That had never really happened before," said Starks. "So this was way outside the normal behavior, and the marketplace really wasn't prepared for that type of a shift and the increase of product coming in."

The freight market has its own pace and pause when it comes to the flow of trade. According to Starks, truck and rail traditionally run at a similar pace: Volumes pick up in the month of March, and then there is an ebb and flow throughout the summer. By October, all the holiday items are in and it is considered the end of the shipping season. November and December are typically slow.

Avery Vise, vice president of trucking research at FTR, described the change: "Instead, we saw an influx of freight during November and December. But the surprise to everyone was that when it came in, the containers didn't move out. Companies just brought in the product and kept it there. This stockpile created a huge disruption in the trucking environment and intermodal and rail."

Warehouses quickly filled up, increasing prices for the precious space.

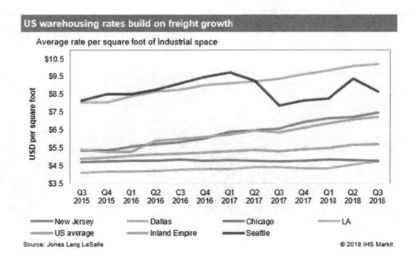

US warehousing rates build on freight growth

Average rate per square foot of industrial space

New Jersey — Dallas — Chicago — LA — US average — Inland Empire — Seattle

Source: Jones Lang LaSalle

© 2018 IHS Markit

Because prices were high and space was tight, intermodal equipment like chassis were transformed into makeshift storage units. The normal turn time for intermodal chassis is approximately three days, but because of businesses holding on to the transmodal equipment, there was a drop in availability, which increased the average turnaround time to approximately six or seven days. The increase was more than double the normal expectation, and that was a shock to the system.[91]

Chassis availability was choked. Traditionally, when a truck arrives at the location to pick up its container, a chassis is available at the same location. But that was no longer a guarantee. The chassis could be on hold and not available, or not be there at all. Because of the shortage, truckers were now faced with what are called "chassis splits"—when a trucker has to drive to a second location to get a chassis. This eats into the drive time, and if there is no chassis available, deliveries are knocked off schedule.

"The hold time was dramatic. Equipment essentially was being held captive," explained Todd Tranausky, vice president for rail and intermodal at FTR. "While the average hold on chassis doubled, in some areas of the marketplace the hold times were even more extreme. We heard of people taking around 70, 80, even 90 days to turn a chassis! It probably was not happening at that level

---

[91] FTR Transportation Intelligence

on a widespread basis, but there were probably places where it was happening. People were using intermodal equipment as storage, and that made it harder for everybody else to get equipment when they needed it."

In an ideal world, according to Weston LaBar, CEO of the Harbor Trucking Association, the entire supply chain would collaborate and coordinate to make sure a moving truck always had a container behind it.[92] There would be no "standby time," during which the truck would have to wait inside a facility to be loaded or unloaded.

"An efficient flow of container movement would mean I'd leave my yard with a container empty or loaded and show up at the terminal within my appointment time to drop-off," said LaBar. "Then another container would be loaded, and I'd leave to my destination. Once I arrived, there would be a space ready for me to drop-off, and I'd pick up another container. It's a continuous movement."

Instead, LaBar continued, "essentially a chassis hoarding situation was created. Many of the cargo owners have provisions in their contracts with ocean carriers called 'free chassis days,' and the cargo owners were using those days and more. The extra waiting time costs the truckers money because they were not moving any containers. Trucking capacity was lost." Because of truck industry safety regulations, truckers are only allowed to work a certain number of hours within a shift and week. That is not fungible. It doesn't matter if the driver is sitting delayed at the terminal or moving on the highway—hours behind the wheel are hours.

The impact of this unintended trade war consequence was simple: Longer waiting periods for both chassis and cargo ate into the movement of the containers. "Instead of a driver moving three containers, they may only be able to move one," said LaBar. "This created an *artificial* trucker shortage. There were enough drivers to move the cargo. It was the *system* that was hindering the process."

---

[92] The Harbor Trucking Association is the nation's largest drayage-specific group and represents employees and contractors from port supply chain trucking companies, marine terminals, beneficial cargo owners, predominantly servicing the West Coast Ports: Seattle, Tacoma, Oakland, Los Angeles, Long Beach. The association does have national membership.

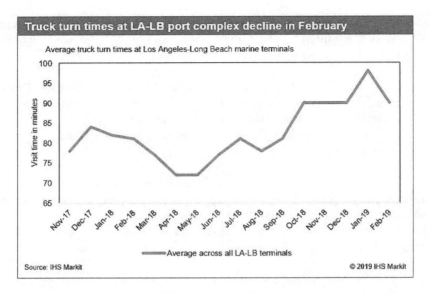

The combination of front-loading and the mobile storage on wheels shrank the capacity to move efficiently. There was more cargo to move with the same number of drivers and less equipment available.

Port Shuffle

Because of the slowdown and the fear of the tariffs looming, some cargo owners (companies) were changing ports to get their products in before the tariffs hit. "We saw a noticeable shift in port activity," said Starks. "We saw a shift from L.A., Long Beach, and movement into the Pacific Northwest or the Gulf and the southeast. It was all about beating the clock."

"The front-loading was a double-edged sword for the intermodal segment," said LaBar. "The surge of cargo helped extend, or extenuate, our peak season, but the problem was, we got flooded with an influx of goods that we were never set up to handle. The port operates much like a funnel," he explained. "You can only pour so much through the gate of a port before you start to get congestion backing up. And that's essentially what happened. We went from having a nice fluid movement of cargo through the gates to having way more cargo than we could ever handle. The ports are only built to handle so much."

In order to avoid the massive bottlenecks and getting smacked with tariffs, the race was on for U.S. importers to flex up volumes to other ports. "If you leverage yourself to one port, then you are putting all your eggs in one basket, and if that port has a hiccup or that port has congestion, there's no easy way out of it," explained Tranausky. "And there's no way to get additional capacity at those other outlets when everybody in that area is looking for the same thing."

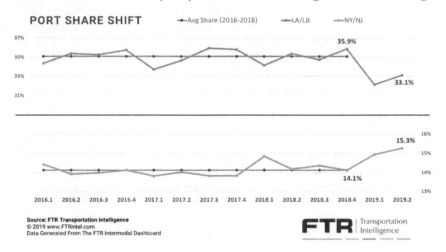

PORT SHARE SHIFT ◆ Avg Share (2016-2018) ◆ LA/LB ◆ NY/NJ

Source: FTR Transportation Intelligence
© 2019 www.FTRintel.com
Data Generated From The FTR Intermodal Dashboard

This is not the first time there has been a shift in the flow of trade through the intermodal system. The protracted labor negotiations in 2014 and 2015 between the International Longshore and Warehouse Union and the Pacific Maritime Association also caused a slowdown on the West Coast, which had some cargo owners moving vessels to other ports to unload their product.[93]

"Seeing cargo owners moving their containers to another port is something we're always sensitive of, because in many cases, when a container leaves the West Coast, it's not coming back, especially if it's discretionary cargo," said LaBar. "We have seen this happen first hand. If it gets diverted to another port, like Houston or the southeast, it's really a decision that is expensive for the cargo owner to make. So they're probably not gonna bring it back to the West Coast. Some of the containers are also diverted to Canada or Mexico because they have capacity available. We saw a lot of cargo shifted to those areas."

"In January and February of 2019, you saw a huge jump in volumes coming into the ports of New York and New Jersey with freight that would have seasonally gone to the ports of L.A. and Long Beach," said Tranausky. "You saw companies move away from the congestion and into other locations, where there was no threat of tariffs. The longer travel time was okay."

---

93   Harbor Trucking Association

The movement of containers to different ports and the stockpile of supply threw off the normal routes of the truckers. Jeff Tucker, CEO of Tucker Company Worldwide, America's oldest privately held freight brokerage company, saw these changes firsthand through the deals he was making. "Motor carriers, when they set up contracts, try to build regularity into their routes and create round trips to maximize profitability, but also to cater to their drivers' needs. They tend to use the same drivers over and over because those drivers become familiar with their route and they know when they can take their breaks, where they can stop overnight, and that planning makes for a smooth freight transport," explained Tucker. "That all changed with the trade war. A lot of the contracts that were considered long-term between the carrier and the shippers were canceled because supply chain routes changed, which created a larger supply of carriers spilling into the spot market. Freight that went into the spot market gave the shippers the leverage and softened the price of freight contracts."

DAT Spot Market Van Volumes & Rates

"The changes in these contracts meant you were no longer handling contract freight in certain lanes, and the drivers were not familiar with the route, pickup, or destination. Drivers don't like that type of uncertainty," said Tucker. "It's a turnoff for drivers, and you run the risk of losing good workers."

Tale of the Containers: China Not Buying

Any negotiation always has an element of "good faith." It shows that the participants are willing. Part of that good intention can be seen in transactions. Since the first tariffs and counter tariffs were levied, the flow of Chinese goods into the United States has continued at a steady pace. However, the flow of U.S. goods going into China has been repeatedly turned on and off. This spigot approach to trade negotiations has resulted in a drastic decrease in U.S. exports to China and a record number of empty containers.

Before the trade war, the import-export balance in U.S. trade with China was around 2:1. That means for every two Chinese containers that were imported, only one U.S. container was exported to China.[94] In 2018, the total number of empty containers handled by the 10 largest container ports in the United States increased by 5.6 percent to a record of 10.89 million TEU (twenty-foot equivalent units), with the handling of these empty containers soaring 25.6 percent.[95] That increased the ratio to approximately 3:1.

"In May of 2019, the Port of Los Angeles reported a record number of container moves," said LaBar. "But the part that's left out is that they were mostly *empty* containers, being returned as part of the import surge. A lot of my members had their drivers busy just taking empties back, and that's not a productive move for anybody. Container moves aside, we want containers *loaded* with exports or imports. We don't want empty containers going either way, and that's what we saw. It's the phenomenon of a lot of gate moves, but mostly with empty cargo."

This phenomenon, LaBar explained, is taking a big bite out of the truck industry's economics. The industry's short-drive category, or drayage, is one of the biggest victims of this imbalance. Drayage thrives on dual trucking transactions, wherein a driver drops off an empty container and picks up a full one. With so many empties, LaBar said, drayage operators in Southern California were faced with a new fiscal problem: Several years ago, they were enjoying a healthy 80 percent in dual transactions, but the tariff war has carved into that number, with dual transactions down to less than 20 percent in 2018.

Because of the wide scope of countries involved in the trade war, the list of U.S. items under retaliatory tariffs continues to grow. Some items are no longer

---

[94]   U.S. Census
[95]   "Alphaliner: Tariffs Intensify U.S. Container Imbalance," World Maritime News, February 18, 2019

exported because of the tariffs. Based on the flow of intermodal trade, the glaring imbalance of the rapid acceleration of Chinese imports and the drastic deceleration of U.S. exports is clear. In 2018, a historic 25 percent drop in U.S. exports to China was recorded.[96]

This drastic decrease of U.S. exports to China continued into 2019. In the first five months of 2019, U.S. exports to China were 18.8 percent year-over-year, for a total of $43 billion. With the front-loading slowing down, Chinese imports reached $180 billion, down 12.2 percent year-over-year.[97]

From the trucker standpoint, with U.S. exports down so much and the export of certain items like recyclables and soybeans almost nonexistent, some carriers were faced with reconsidering what freight they could move in order to stay afloat.

"Drivers might now be forced to move 'unattractive' freight," said Tucker. "Meaning freight that is dirtier, maybe requires slightly different equipment; it could also mean the job requires you to wash out the trailer before pickup. Invariably, it also means moving lower-priced freight. The one who is going to get hurt here is the little guy—the people who mortgaged their house several times to set up their business. It's survival of the fittest, and you need to have certainty to plan, and right now, with this trade war, there is none. The environment is murky."

The imbalance of trade begs the question: Just how committed are the Chinese to reaching a trade deal if they are *not* increasing their U.S. exports?

---

[96]   Port of Los Angeles, PIERS, IHS Markit
[97]   "Economics and Trade Bulletin," U.S.-China Economic and Security Commission, July 3, 2019

Figure 1: U.S. Exports, Imports, and the Trade Deficit with China, January 2018–May 2019

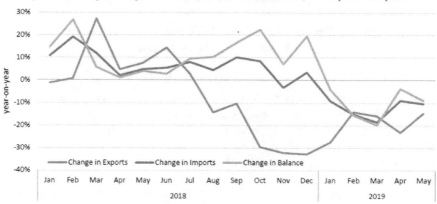

Source: U.S. Census Bureau, Trade in Goods with China, July 3, 2019. *https://www.census.gov/foreign-trade/balance/c5700.html.*

"The intermodal flow of U.S. exports to China is the exclamation point to the unintended consequences of this trade war," said LaBar. "How can we be 'winning' when we are seeing record declines?"

CHAPTER SEVEN

If the Trade Wars End, Will the Flow of Trade Go Back to the Way It Was?

Based on the indisputable proof of the physical flow of containers, cargo, and tankers, the United States' trade war against its various trading partners has altered the global pattern of trade. The ever-growing list of tariffs imposed by the United States and the retaliatory tariffs have clogged, rerouted, removed, or in some cases expanded the flow of trade.

The maritime industry provides the global economy with the elasticity to grow and become more interconnected. With 90 percent of the world's trade transported by water, the flow of maritime trade has been a catalyst for prosperity and contagion, which have influenced the global economy. Trade is influenced by optimism, uncertainty, and fear. These emotions can have either a chilling or an energizing impact on capital spending, which influences growth. The flow of trade will continue to change as the escalation of tariffs between the United States and China reaches new heights.

The history of both countries is steeped in a culture of not backing down. In the negotiation arena, it's in shades of gray that compromises are met. In a black-and-white world, agreements are not reached.

China's sustainability philosophy is the foundation of its trade negotiation strategy. Xi's speech before the first China International Export Expo, in November 2018, supported this notion that China will not make significant concessions. "Great winds and storms may upset a pond, but not an ocean," Xi said, comparing China to a vast and immovable sea. "After 5,000 years of trials and tribulations, China is still here. Looking ahead, China will be here to stay.... As globalization deepens, the practices of law of jungle and winner-take-all are a dead end."[98]

During the course of the trade war, China has expanded its resources for energy and agricultural products with other countries to diversify its import portfolio and cut out the United States where it can. China's pursuit and completion of deals are an essential part of its Belt Road Initiative and Xi's long-term trade

---

[98] Keynote speech by President Xi Jinping at the opening ceremony of the first China International Import Expo, November 5, 2018, Xinhua

vision of a self-reliant country. The long-term goals of China supersede any negative short-term impact the country might face.

Trade War Tirade

Fear and anger swept through the markets on August 23, 2019, when the Chinese government responded to the United States' September 1 tariffs with retaliatory measures of its own. A new round of tariffs on $75 billion worth of U.S. products, including oil, would be applied, along with the reapplying of duties on American autos. The tariffs would come in two batches: the first in September, and the second on December 15, just like the United States tariff measures. The range imposed on U.S. exports would span from 5 percent to 10 percent on the $75 billion of U.S. goods. The December 15 phase of the tariffs would hit the U.S. automotive sector with a 25 percent tariff on U.S. cars and a 5 percent tariff on auto parts and components.

"In response to the measures by the U.S., China was forced to take countermeasures," Chinese State Council said in a statement. "The Chinese side hopes that the U.S. will continue to follow the consensus of the Osaka meeting, return to the correct track of consultation and resolve differences, and work hard with China to end the goal of ending economic and trade frictions."[99]

The timing of China's retaliatory announcement left no opportunity for U.S. companies to export their products in before the September 1 tariffs were imposed. The December 15 date, however, would give companies from other countries time to front-load products in. President Trump blasted back in a flurry of tweets.

While tweets condemning the tariffs are something the global markets have seen, President Trump's ordering U.S. companies out of China was not. The "order" sent the markets spiraling down 600 points and raised the question if President Trump would indeed declare a national emergency under a 1977 law called the International Emergency Economic Powers Act, or IEEPA. If the president declared such an emergency, it would give him the power to stop companies or entire sectors from conducting activities with China. Past presidents have invoked the law, such as when Jimmy Carter did so to freeze foreign governments' assets in the Iran sanctions.

---

[99] The State Council Tariff Commission issued a notice to determine the tariffs on the recovery of automobiles and parts originating in the United States, August 23, 2019

Donald J. Trump ✔ @realDonaldTrump

Our Country has lost, stupidly, Trillions of Dollars with China over many years. They have stolen our Intellectual Property at a rate of Hundreds of Billions of Dollars a year, & they want to continue. I won't let that happen! We don't need China and, frankly, would be far....

10:59 AM · Aug 23, 2019 · Twitter for iPhone

12.2K Retweets   **41.6K** Likes

Donald J. Trump ✔ @realDonaldTrump · 1h
Replying to @realDonaldTrump
....better off without them. The vast amounts of money made and stolen by China from the United States, year after year, for decades, will and must STOP. Our great American companies are hereby ordered to immediately start looking for an alternative to China, including bringing..

5.3K   5.2K   17.3K

Donald J. Trump ✔ @realDonaldTrump · 1h
....your companies HOME and making your products in the USA. I will be responding to China's Tariffs this afternoon. This is a GREAT opportunity for the United States. Also, I am ordering all carriers, including Fed Ex, Amazon, UPS and the Post Office, to SEARCH FOR & REFUSE,....

Donald J. Trump ✔ @realDonaldTrump · 1h
....all deliveries of Fentanyl from China (or anywhere else!). Fentanyl kills 100,000 Americans a year. President Xi said this would stop - it didn't. Our Economy, because of our gains in the last 2 1/2 years, is MUCH larger than that of China. We will keep it that way!

5.8K   8.5K   32.1K

In the late afternoon, once the markets closed for the day for trading, President Trump announced a revised set of tariffs. On September 1, the $300 billion dollars of goods and products from China would be taxed at 15 percent, versus the 10 percent originally declared; and starting on October 15, the 250 billion dollars of goods and products from China currently taxed at 25 percent would be increased to 30 percent. Originally this tariff was set to go into effect October 1, but President Trump delayed the increase in a gesture of goodwill toward China.

Responses from the American business community were sharp and swift. In a statement, David French, senior vice president of government affairs for the National Retail Federation, said, "It's impossible for businesses to plan for the future in this type of environment.... The administration's approach clearly isn't working, and the answer isn't more taxes on American businesses and consumers. Where does this end?"[100]

Timeline of U.S.-China Trade Tensions, 2018–2019

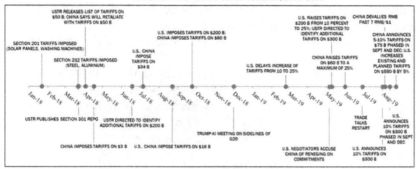

Source: Adapted from Chad Bown and Melina Kolb, "Trump's Trade War Timeline: An Up-to-Date Guide," *Peterson Institute for International Economics*, August 23, 2019. https://www.piie.com/blogs/trade-investment-policy-watch/trump-trade-war-china-date-guide. U.S.-China Economic and Security Review Commission

At the G-7 meeting in France, President Trump told reporters he regretted he hadn't raised the tariffs higher on China. The escalated trade war with China continued to mushroom, taking away the spotlight from a positive trade development with Japan announced at the meeting of world leaders. The U.S. and Japan had agreed in principle to core elements of a trade deal that would include agriculture, industrial tariffs, and digital trade. The Japanese markets would be open to U.S. goods and lead to a substantial reduction in tariffs items including beef. Japan still faces U.S. tariffs on its own auto exports, so the details are still being worked out. The two countries hoped to ink an official deal at United Nations meetings at the end of September.

Tariff Trickle-Down Effect

The health of the Chinese economy is crucial to the flow of trade because of the tremendous volumes of trade that flow into and out of the country. Because of the tariffs, the country has seen a steady movement of American companies leaving and setting up manufacturing plants in countries like Vietnam to avoid the tariffs. These plant closings have had a negative impact on the Chinese economy. The slowing has created an economic undertow that has expanded from China to the U.S. trading partners.

In August 2019, global economic softness hit the United States. The U.S. manufacturing purchasing managers' index (PMI) data showed that

---

[100] "Retailers Respond to Tariff Escalation: 'Where Does This End?'" National Retail Federation, August 23, 2019

manufacturing new orders had dropped to the lowest in 10 years and export sales sunk to the lowest level since the Great Recession (2008–2009). Steel and aluminum companies, which rely on a healthy economy, were already forecasting a drop in orders. This was something not even the 232 could shield them from. No tariffs are impervious to the dynamics of supply and demand. The flow of the cargo shows the drop in steel demand on the global stage.

The boomerang effect of the tariffs can be seen in the agriculture sector, which is a large consumer of steel and aluminum. Without the extra discretionary spending money, the farmer is not reinvesting in new machinery. In a third-quarter conference call, John Deere's CFO Ryan Campbell explained to analysts that the company would be holding back expansion plans because the U.S.-China trade war, the harsh weather, and the loss of livestock to disease had all negatively impacted global agriculture. "North American customer sentiment has since deteriorated not only due to uncertainty over market access, but also due to weather and the demand impact of African swine fever," Campbell says. "As these challenges persist, we are now beginning more aggressive action on our cost structure to create a more efficient and nimble organization."

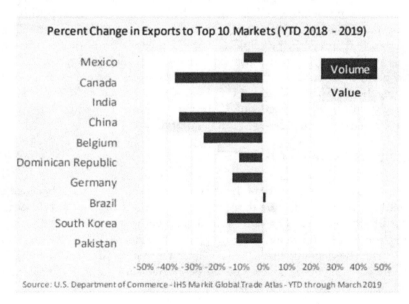

Despite the headwinds facing the steel industry and U.S. Steel's announcement in June that it would idle two plants because of softening demand and lower steel prices, President Trump declared before a packed audience in Pennsylvania on August 13, 2019, that his tariff on steel and aluminum had turned around the steel industry, transforming it from a "dead" business into a "thriving" sector.[101] Three days later, on August 19, U.S. Steel officially announced the temporary layoff of 200 workers at its Great Lakes facility in Michigan. According to U.S. Steel, the layoffs could last longer than six months. These layoffs were expected—the company had first announced them in its second-quarter earnings call—but that did not stop the ensuing debate on the effectiveness of the 232 on steel.

Rhetoric of that debate aside, based on the flow of trade, the 232 continues to do what it was intended to do. U.S. imports of steel are down. Through the first seven months of 2019, finished steel imports were down 10.6 percent—and down 16.4 percent versus the same time frame in 2018.[102]

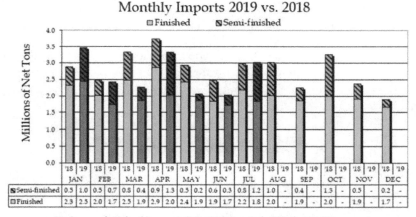

Monthly Imports 2019 vs. 2018

% change finished imports July 2019 vs. July 2018 -15.7%

Source: American Iron and Steel Institute

Finished import market share year-to-date was 21 percent.

---

[101]   Remarks by President Trump on American Energy and Manufacturing, Monaca, PA, August 13, 2019

[102]   "Steel Imports Down 11 Percent Year-to-Date Through July," American Iron and Steel Institute, August 23, 2019

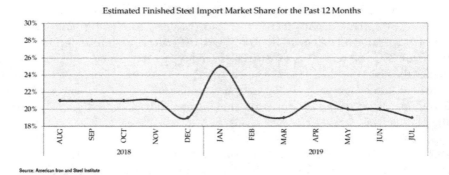

Estimated Finished Steel Import Market Share for the Past 12 Months

Source: American Iron and Steel Institute

"Goodwill" Versus "True Intent"

Many times China has promised to buy large quantities of U.S. agricultural products. The number one indicator of the progress of those talks is the amount of U.S. exports being purchased and transported, and U.S. exports to China continue to decrease. This slowdown indicates that the olive branches being offered by the Chinese have borne little fruit when it comes to reaching a trade deal.

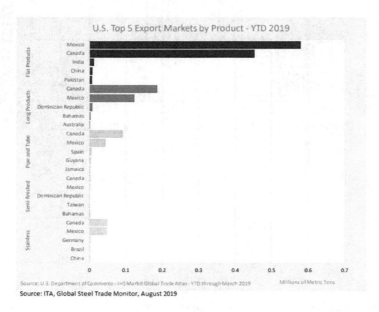

Source: ITA, Global Steel Trade Monitor, August 2019

The slowdown in China is impeding the efforts on the Trump administration's goal of decreasing the United States' trade deficit. In the first half of 2019, the deficit climbed to a 10-year high. According to the data from the Bureau of Economic Analysis, the trade deficit in goods and services brought the half-year total to $316 billion, the highest since 2008. One of the biggest factors contributing to the historically high deficit was the trade of goods. That amounted to a record $439 billion; $219 billion could be traced back to the China trade deficit.

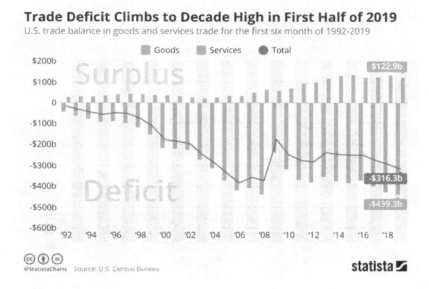

Trade Deficit Climbs to Decade High in First Half of 2019
U.S. trade balance in goods and services trade for the first six month of 1992-2019

From the massive pullback in energy and agriculture buys to the inking of energy deals with Russia and Qatar, China's various responses to the trade war bring to mind the advice our parents gave: Actions speak louder than words. Are China's actions really in line with its promises to work out a trade resolution with the United States? The proof is in the flow of trade, and the result of the growing trade gap with the United States based on that physical movement of trade is clear.

The on-again, off-again U.S.-China trade discussions have injected hope and fear into the investing community too many times to count. Words are a powerful tool in negotiations. Yet the goodwill promises being made by the Chinese have been found hollow. How do you measure the vast emptiness behind those pledges and promises? By looking at the volumes being transported by tankers and container and cargo vessels. In the end, U.S. export volumes to China have contradicted the rhetoric of deal negotiations and the United States "winning." For example, if China truly wanted to make up for its diminished 2018 soybean purchases, it would have to *triple* its purchases in 2019.[103]

Little impact
Rising tariffs between the United States and China
have had a limited effect on the trade balance
between both countries.
(China trade balance with US, billions of US dollars, 12-month moving sum)

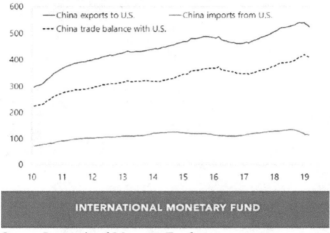

Source: International Monetary Fund

The reality of China's commitment to buying the U.S. 2019 crop is dim. "The current marketing year has seen both sales and exports to China, although well below what is typical," explained American Farm Bureau Federation economist Michael Nepveux. "There were several weeks during which no orders were placed. Typically, by now, you would see several orders for the next marketing year placed. For example, at this time in 2017, there were about 2.8 MMT [million metric tons] in outstanding sales to China for the '17–'18 marketing year. There are virtually no sales to China for the 2019 marketing year."

After China's Commerce Ministry announced on August 5 that Chinese companies would stop buying U.S. farm products, two deals were made: a small amount of soybeans (9,589 tons), and one cargo with approximately 66,000 tons for next year.[104]

---

[103]   Farm Bureau
[104]   USDA, August 9–15, 2019

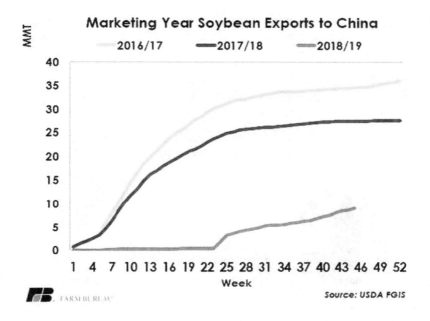

Marketing Year Soybean Exports to China

Source: USDA FGIS

It was a puzzling development in this trade war. Terry Reilly, senior commodity analyst for Futures International, told Reuters, "The government may have just given the green light to say, 'Let this one go through,'" Reilly said. "One cargo is not going to change the fact that they're not buying millions of tons of soybeans."[105]

Change in Trade Routes

Warnings of the negative consequences of the trade war were sounded by economists and maritime experts as soon as the bluster of the threats began. In a June 2018 report, Peter Sand wrote of the negative consequences a multiple-front trade war would have on global growth: "From a wider perspective, the effect of an escalating trade war may derail the current global upswing, which is at its highest point since 2011 and expected to continue. This will have cascading effects on shipping demand as a whole. Free trade provides prosperity and is a fundamental principle to cherish and safeguard."

The changes in the flow of trade have impacted forecasts in global growth. The economists at the IMF have had to take out their erasers several times to revise

---

[105] Tom Polansek, "China Buys U.S. Soybeans After Declaring Ban on American Farm Goods," Reuters, August 22, 2019

their 2019 global GDP growth downward since their first 2019 forecast, in July of 2018. At that time, the two largest trading partners in the world were newly locked in the trade dispute.

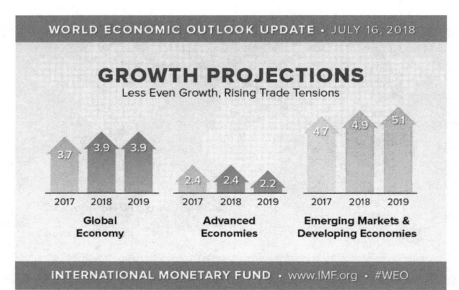

Source: "2019 World Economic Outlook Update,"
International Monetary Fund, July 16, 2018

The IMF's initial forecast for 2019 was 3.9 percent GDP growth. A year later, with additional tariffs and retaliatory tariffs levied, the IMF revised global GDP down to 3.2 percent.[106] According to a July 2019 report, "Dynamism in the global economy is being weighed down by prolonged policy uncertainty as trade tensions remain heightened despite the recent U.S.-China trade truce, technology tensions have erupted threatening global technology supply chains, and the prospects of a no-deal Brexit have increased."[107]

Describing the sluggish growth as "self-inflicted," the IMF reported that "global trade growth, which moves closely with investment, has slowed significantly to 0.5 percent (year-over-year) in the first quarter of 2019, which is its slowest pace since 2012."[108]

---

[106] "World Economic Outlook Update," International Monetary Fund, July 23, 2019

[107] Gita Gopinath, "Sluggish Global Growth Calls for Supportive Policies," IMFBlog, International Monetary Fund, July 23, 2019

[108] Gopinath, "Sluggish Global Growth"

Source: "2019 World Economic Outlook," International Monetary Fund, July 2019

Multifront Trade War

The tremendous volumes of Chinese exports entering the United States shifted the flow of trade to the ports in the east, which then trickled down to the roads and bridges.

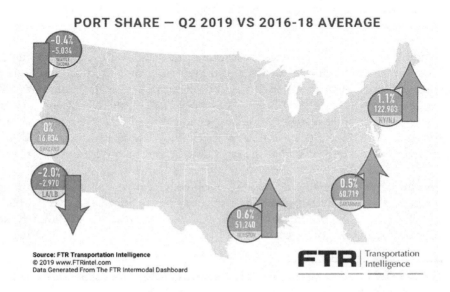

Source: FTR Transportation Intelligence
© 2019 www.FTRintel.com
Data Generated From The FTR Intermodal Dashboard

The trade war with China was not the only factor in the movement of cargo at the ports. The retaliatory tariffs slapped back by the European Union, Russia, India, Turkey, Canada, and Mexico in response to the tariffs on steel, aluminum, solar panels, and washing machines also contributed to the change in trade flow. The tariffs levied by Canada and Mexico were on from July 1, 2018, to May 20, 2019, when the United States reached a deal with both countries to sell steel and aluminum in the United States without major tariffs. That opened a trade pipe that had been closed off. This deal also helped pave the way for the countries to ratify the United States–Mexico–Canada Agreement (USMCA).

The trade war with the E.U. has global economists and market watchers worried. According to the trade data from the USTR, the United States imported $683 billion from the E.U., compared to the $557.9 billion from China. What has been most concerning to the global markets is the amount of goods and services the United States exports to the E.U.: $574.5 billion versus the $179.2 billion exported to China. The U.S.-E.U. trade flow is far larger than the trade flow between the United States and China. At a campaign rally in New Hampshire on August 15, 2019, Trump said the E.U. was "worse than China, just smaller," and that "it treats us horribly—barriers, tariffs, taxes—and we let them come in." At the G-7, French President Emmanuel Macron announced at the U.S.-France joint press conference and on Twitter that he and President Trump would be working together on an agreement to modernize international tax rules on digital companies. The product in the tariff crosshairs for the digital taxation on U.S. companies was French wine. President Trump at the G-7 press conference did not answer a French reporter's question if a deal had indeed been made.[109]

In addition to the possible tariffs on wine in retaliation to the tech tax, the 232 on autos assembled in the E.U. is also on the table, as well as proposed tax on specialty foods. The food tariff would be in response to the multiyear WTO dispute between Airbus and Boeing. On April 8, 2019, the USTR announced it was "initiating an investigation under Section 301 of the Trade Act 1974 to enforce the United States' rights in the World Trade Organization dispute involving subsidies provided to the large civil aircraft by the European Union."

This important bilateral trade flow pipe is already being constricted with the 232 steel and aluminum retaliation. The retaliatory tariffs priced out over $3 billion of U.S. goods. One hundred and eighty types of products, including whiskey, navy beans, and motorcycles, were hit hard. Looking at trade as a percentage of

---

[109] G-7 U.S., France Press Conference, August 26, 2019. "I can confirm that the first lady loved your French wine," President Trump said.

GDP, the E.U. tops China. The tariffs on the E.U. have created an obstruction in the pipes of trade between the two markets. The trade deficit between the E.U. and the U.S. in the first half of 2019 rose more than 9 percent (approximately $83 billion) when compared to the retaliatory tariffs which were imposed in 2018.[110] This goods trade deficit has steadily widened through the years. The deficit in 2018 was $169.3 billion, which was an 11.8 percent increase ($17.9 billion) over 2017. Over 2008, the U.S. trade deficit with E.U. increased 77.1 percent.[111]

Trade (% of GDP)

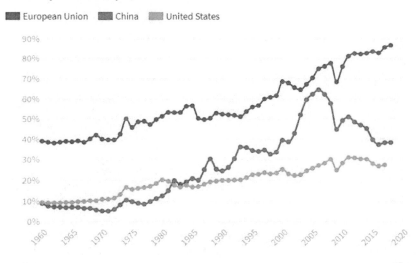

Source: The World Bank

The E.U. tariffs were not the only ones levied on the U.S. in retaliation for the 232 on steel and aluminum. India also slapped tariffs on American goods. Originally, India was going to set a tariff as high as 70 percent on $235 million of U.S. goods such as apples and almonds. India is the largest consumer of U.S. almonds and the second largest buyer of apples. Trade talks were delayed so both countries could negotiate. Talks did not bring a solution, and India increased its tariff list by $5 million. On June 16, 2019, India finally imposed a tariff of 70 percent on $240 million of U.S. product.

---

[110]   Department of Commerce, 2019
[111]   USTR, European Union Trade explainer, 2019

India's retaliation against US exports mainly hits fruits and nuts from California and Washington state

US exports to India subject to India's retaliatory tariffs on June 16, 2019, millions of dollars

Source: Figure 3 from "Trump's Mini-Trade War With India," by Chad P. Bown, PIIE Trade and Investment Policy Watch, originally published by the Peterson Institute for International Economics on July 8, 2019. (https://www.piie.com/blogs/trade-and-investment-policy-watch/trumps-mini-trade-warindia)

In his tough trade talk at the rally in Pennsylvania, President Trump declared that India and China should have their "developing country" classification removed.[112] President Trump has in the past labeled India an "import tariff king" and threatened the country with a Section 301 probe.

Trade between India and the United States more than doubled between 2008 and 2018, to over $10 billion. The United States is the largest export destination for India and its second largest trading partner. Still, India's surplus of $20 billion with the U.S. does not compare to China's trade surplus of over $400 billion.

Navigating the Bluster

The escalation of trade rhetoric has created a cloak of uncertainty that has some businesses either shelving or changing plans because of the risk. "The trade for aluminum has just completely changed," said shipping logistics expert Anton Posner. "Even though Turkey is back to a 25 percent tariff [the same as Italy], Turkish business has not come back because traders are nervous given all the

---

[112] Remarks by President Trump on American Energy and Manufacturing, Monaca, PA, August 13, 2019

turmoil with the U.S. and Turkey; the possibility of more sanctions and penalties being levied on Turkey is a real concern. So if a trader rolls the dice and starts business with Turkish steel mills again, it could jeopardize the trading company if the U.S. hits back at Turkey due to geopolitical events. Because of this, we have seen the trade completely shift to E.U./Italy origin."

Aluminum and steel are not the only areas where the flow of trade has shifted. There have been reports of companies in other industries moving their manufacturing plants out of China to countries like Germany and Vietnam in order to avoid tariffs, and the transpacific data reflects this change.

Southeast Asian nations like Vietnam are becoming the new manufacturing hubs for American businesses seeking to avoid tariffs. In May 2019, Williams-Sonoma's CEO told CNBC that the company had moved some furniture production out of China to countries including Indonesia, Vietnam, and the United States in anticipation of additional tariffs.[113] In December 2018, the company announced it would open a manufacturing facility that would produce upholstered furniture in Tupelo, Mississippi—a move that would create hundreds of jobs in the United States.

"Williams-Sonoma is a great example of how companies are revamping their manufacturing chain and moving out of China," said Ocean Audit's Steve Ferreira. "Additional tariff threats are very real, so companies need to look long-term. The manufacturing and transportation of product overseas is not quick. There is a buying process that goes on between a producer, an exporter, an importer, and a buyer, and that can take from one to three months. Then you have the shipping process, and that physical travel takes several weeks. Given the length of time behind this production, in today's tariff environment, companies need to plan ahead if they can."

The migration of imports can be seen in the data from the first six months of 2019. There was a decline of Chinese imports by 5 percent compared to 2018, while imports from Vietnam were up 30.5 percent.[114] Overall U.S. imports originating from Southeast Asia in the first half of 2019 were up 23.1 percent compared to 2018.[115]

---

[113]   May 13, 2019
[114]   PIERS, IHS Markit
[115]   PIERS, IHS Markit

Direct exports from China to U.S. fall, while exports via Vietnam, Taiwan and Mexico rise

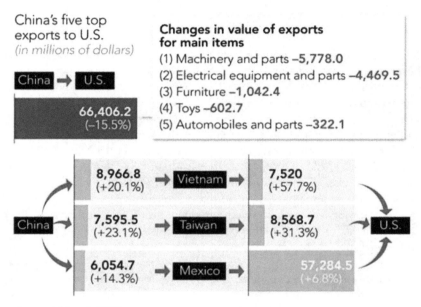

China's five top exports to U.S.
(in millions of dollars)

China → U.S.

66,406.2
(–15.5%)

Changes in value of exports for main items
(1) Machinery and parts –5,778.0
(2) Electrical equipment and parts –4,469.5
(3) Furniture –1,042.4
(4) Toys –602.7
(5) Automobiles and parts –322.1

China →

8,966.8 (+20.1%) → Vietnam → 7,520 (+57.7%)

7,595.5 (+23.1%) → Taiwan → 8,568.7 (+31.3%) → U.S.

6,054.7 (+14.3%) → Mexico → 57,284.5 (+6.8%)

January-March 2019
Source: Data analysis from the U.S. International Trade Commission and the International Trade Centre

Source: *Nikkei Asian Review*, June 01, 2019

Other Southeast Asian countries have also had robust trade growth with the United States: Cambodia saw an increase of 38.3 percent; Malaysia, 22 percent; Thailand, 19.6 percent; and Indonesia, 11.5 percent.[116] This surge of front-loading was easily tracked.

But Vietnam's winning position in the U.S.-China trade war could be short-lived. President Trump said in a June interview, "A lot of companies are moving to Vietnam, but Vietnam takes advantage of us even worse than China. It's almost the single worst abuser of everybody."[117] In May, the U.S. Treasury listed Vietnam as a possible currency manipulator, and a new 456 percent U.S. duty on Vietnamese steel imports that originate from Taiwan and South Korea was imposed by the U.S. Commerce Department in July. Some economists predict

---

[116] PIERS, IHS Markit
[117] Fox Business, June 26, 2019

that the United States will impose a 25 percent tariff on all Vietnamese imports, or tariffs on specific Vietnamese imports, based on accusations of Hanoi allowing transshipment.

Monthly retail imports 2018-2019
(TEU - Millions)

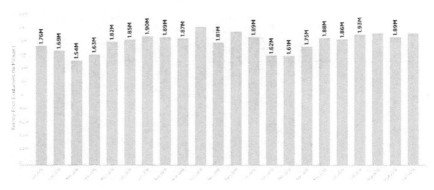

NRF RETAIL

There are two sides to the trade-war coin: on one, U.S. imports; the other, U.S. Exports. In 2018, U.S. exports were down 3.87 percent. Now, more than a year into the trade war, U.S. companies have been successful in expanding their sales in other markets in order to make up for the hole created by the lack of China sales. Compared to 2018, in the first six months of 2019 national U.S. exports to the world are up 1.58 percent.[118] The national export volume is a good indicator that U.S. businesses, and farmers are expanding sales into new markets. But China not fully participating in U.S. trade is a multibillion-dollar missed opportunity.

The following chart shows the trade gaps among U.S. trading partners. All major trading partners of the United States had a trade deficit. These trading partners either have tariffs levied against them or are threatened with the imposition of tariffs.

Tracking the Container Change

One key trade-flow indicator maritime experts and world economists examine is the volume of the eastbound transpacific trade lane (the regional trade lane for ocean containers that originates in East Asia and ends in the United States).

---

[118]   Port of Los Angeles, PIERS, IHS Markit

This trade route is the most important trade pipe for U.S. importers. Over 20 million 20-foot containers have moved each year since 2012.[119] No other trade lane for containers can match that volume. This trade lane accounts for 40 percent of the world's GDP.[120] The flow of these trade pipes offers keen insight into the health of trade talks.

Exhibit 4. Exports, Imports, and Trade Balance of Goods by Country and Area, Not Seasonally Adjusted: 2019

In millions of dollars. Details may not equal totals due to rounding. The countries in this exhibit are ranked by year-to-date totals. (X) Not applicable (-) Represents zero or less than one-half unit of measurement shown.

Country	Balance (Customs imports)			Exports (Domestic & Foreign, F.A.S. basis)			Imports Customs basis			Imports C.I.F. basis		
	May	Year-to-Date	Rank	May	Year-to-Date	Rank	May	Year-to-Date	Rank	May	Year-to-Date	Rank
Africa	-923.6	-1,970.4	(X)	2,410.2	10,903.3	(X)	3,333.8	12,873.7	(X)	3,439.4	13,315.0	(X)
APEC	-58,585.5	-263,877.8	(X)	86,694.2	414,271.1	(X)	145,279.7	678,148.9	(X)	149,368.5	897,810.9	(X)
ASEAN	-9,713.4	-45,743.7	(X)	7,278.7	35,490.0	(X)	16,992.1	81,233.8	(X)	17,569.1	83,935.6	(X)
Asia - South	-3,360.2	-13,799.4	(X)	3,443.5	17,340.1	(X)	6,803.7	31,139.4	(X)	7,061.0	32,342.2	(X)
Asia Near East	334.3	1,774.8	(X)	5,394.8	25,861.7	(X)	5,060.5	24,086.9	(X)	5,190.4	24,781.5	(X)
CAFTA-DR	449.6	3,272.6	(X)	2,758.5	13,801.4	(X)	2,308.9	10,528.8	(X)	2,412.5	11,039.5	(X)
Central American Common Market	201.6	1,608.4	(X)	2,000.5	9,881.6	(X)	1,798.9	8,273.2	(X)	1,888.2	8,715.9	(X)
Euro Area	-15,005.0	-62,565.7	(X)	21,431.2	105,245.5	(X)	36,436.2	167,811.2	(X)	37,186.2	171,315.9	(X)
Europe	-20,680.3	-86,556.0	(X)	32,713.8	161,785.1	(X)	53,394.1	248,341.1	(X)	54,603.2	254,037.6	(X)
European Union	-17,166.2	-69,840.3	(X)	28,352.1	142,581.4	(X)	45,518.3	212,421.6	(X)	46,495.2	217,014.4	(X)
LAFTA	-7,543.2	-32,265.6	(X)	31,281.5	150,365.3	(X)	38,824.7	182,630.9	(X)	39,401.2	185,644.7	(X)
NATO Allies	-13,692.0	-49,091.2	(X)	53,905.6	262,610.0	(X)	67,597.6	311,701.2	(X)	69,167.5	319,238.9	(X)
North America	-12,969.1	-47,392.4	(X)	48,413.4	232,101.0	(X)	61,382.5	279,493.4	(X)	62,313.4	284,025.6	(X)
OECD	-38,712.8	-165,494.3	(X)	96,031.1	463,463.9	(X)	134,743.8	628,958.1	(X)	137,397.5	641,859.9	(X)
OPEC	-155.8	-16.3	(X)	4,484.6	21,229.4	(X)	4,640.5	21,245.7	(X)	4,808.0	22,080.4	(X)
Pacific Rim Countries	-39,034.9	-184,024.2	(X)	33,741.8	159,783.3	(X)	72,776.7	343,807.5	(X)	75,456.5	356,493.1	(X)
South/Central America	4,424.8	20,333.5	(X)	14,045.1	67,277.9	(X)	9,620.5	46,944.5	(X)	10,044.2	49,230.9	(X)
Twenty Latin American Republics	-6,503.6	-25,615.0	(X)	34,785.6	168,159.3	(X)	41,289.2	193,774.3	(X)	41,974.3	197,316.1	(X)

* Countries denoted by asterisks represent countries with Free Trade Agreements with the United States.
** Countries denoted by double asterisks represent countries included within Free Trade Agreements with the United States.

Africa - Algeria, Angola, Benin, Botswana, British Indian Ocean Territories, Burkina Faso, Burundi, Cameroon, Cabo Verde, Central African Republic, Chad, Comoros, Congo (Brazzaville), Congo (Kinshasa), Cote d'Ivoire, Djibouti, Egypt, Equatorial Guinea, Eritrea, Eswatini, Ethiopia, French Southern and Antarctic Lands, Gabon, Gambia, Ghana, Guinea, Guinea-Bissau, Kenya, Lesotho, Liberia, Libya, Madagascar, Malawi, Mali, Mauritania, Mauritius, Mayotte, Morocco, Mozambique, Namibia, Niger, Nigeria, Reunion, Rwanda, Sao Tome and Principe, Senegal, Seychelles, Sierra Leone, Somalia, South Africa, South Sudan, St. Helena, Sudan, Tanzania, Togo, Tunisia, Uganda, Western Sahara, Zambia, Zimbabwe.

APEC (Asia - Pacific Economic Cooperation) - Australia, Brunei, Canada, Chile, China, Hong Kong, Indonesia, Japan, Korea (South), Malaysia, Mexico, New Zealand, Papua New Guinea, Peru, Philippines, Russia, Singapore, Taiwan, Thailand, Vietnam.

ASEAN (Association of Southeast Asian Nations) - Brunei, Burma, Cambodia, Indonesia, Laos, Malaysia, Philippines, Singapore, Thailand, Vietnam.

Asia - South - Afghanistan, Bangladesh, India, Nepal, Pakistan, Sri Lanka.

Asia Near East - Bahrain, Gaza Strip Administered by Israel, Iran, Iraq, Israel, Jordan, Kuwait, Lebanon, Oman, Qatar, Saudi Arabia, Syria, United Arab Emirates, West Bank Administered by Israel, Yemen.

CAFTA-DR (Dominican Republic-Central America-United States Free Trade Agreement) - Costa Rica, Dominican Republic, El Salvador, Guatemala, Honduras, Nicaragua.

Central American Common Market - Costa Rica, El Salvador, Guatemala, Honduras, Nicaragua.

Euro Area - Austria, Belgium, Cyprus, Estonia, Finland, France, Germany, Greece, Ireland, Italy, Latvia, Lithuania, Luxembourg, Malta, Netherlands, Portugal, Slovakia, Slovenia, Spain.

Europe - Albania, Andorra, Armenia, Austria, Azerbaijan, Belarus, Belgium, Bosnia-Herzegovina, Bulgaria, Croatia, Cyprus, Czech Republic, Denmark, Estonia, Faroe Islands, Finland, France, Georgia, Germany, Gibraltar, Greece, Hungary, Iceland, Ireland, Italy, Kazakhstan, Kosovo, Kyrgyzstan, Latvia, Liechtenstein, Lithuania, Luxembourg, Malta, Moldova, Monaco, Montenegro, North Macedonia, Norway, Poland, Portugal, Romania, Russia, San Marino, Serbia, Slovakia, Slovenia, Spain, Svalbard, Jan Mayen Island, Sweden, Switzerland, Tajikistan, Turkey, Turkmenistan, Ukraine, United Kingdom, Uzbekistan, Vatican City.

European Union - Austria, Belgium, Bulgaria, Croatia, Cyprus, Czech Republic, Estonia, Finland, France, Germany, Greece, Hungary, Ireland, Italy, Latvia, Lithuania, Luxembourg, Malta, Netherlands, Poland, Portugal, Romania, Slovakia, Slovenia, Spain, Sweden, United Kingdom.

Source: U.S. Census

In container shipping, this trade is looked at from two different pipes. The "fronthaul" pipe, which is the route from China to the United States, and the "backhaul" pipe, which is U.S. exports to China. Because the United States has always imported more from China than it exports to China, the fronthaul pipe has always been more profitable for the shipping industry because of the higher container volume.

This volume dictates shipping capacity. The equation is simple supply and demand: When more containers need to be moved, more ships are needed to move them. If, for some reason, the fronthaul volumes go down, fewer ships

---

[119] FreightWaves
[120] Council of Foreign Relations

are needed to move them, and that drops the price because there are more ships than the supply requires. This then impacts the pricing of short-term vessel contracts known as the spot rate. Because of the continuous uncertainty being created by the trade war, spot rates have been driven up.

Sand warned about this impact before the trade war even started, in that June 2018 report. "The shipping industry is concerned with a lower level of U.S. containerized imports which may become a result of a trade war between the U.S. and China. If fronthaul volumes go down, oversupply of ships develops causing utilization to drop alongside freight rates and earnings on the transpacific networks in many aspects, backhaul shipments only serve to cover a part of the repositioning costs of a ship to the next fronthaul voyage—they don't generate profits."

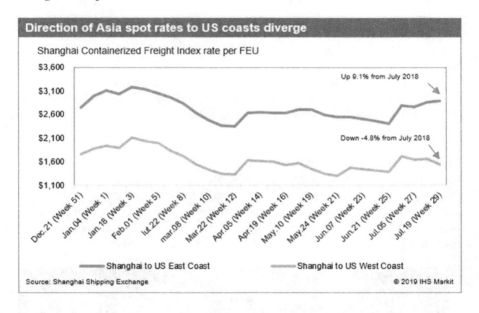

Blue Water Reporting's capacity report breaks down and compares the capacity disparity created by the trade war: "Between May 2017 and May 2018, estimated allocated TEUs on the trade *increased* 11.4 percent, from 397,419 TEUs to 442,858 TEUs. In contrast, between May 2018 and May 2019, estimated weekly allocated TEUs on the trade *dropped* 5.1 percent, from 442,858 TEUs to 420,430 TEUs."[121]

---

[121]   Henry Byers, "Container Rate Increases Are Expected on the Trans-Pacific Eastbound," *American Shipper*, Blue Water, June 2019

Figure 1: U.S. Exports, Imports, and the Trade Deficit with China, January 2018–May 2019

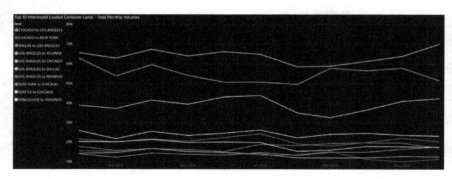

The change in the flow of containers from East Asia to the Port of Los Angeles has caused historic disruptions. The longer the trade war continues, said Gene Seroka, the more erectable harm is caused. "Money is on the sidelines because of this uncertainty," Seroka stressed. "Whether it's companies that traditionally invest or using capital to update their facilities or hire more folks, capital creates more R&D dollars. With money not being invested, it is not good over the long term."

The changes in trade have led to the modulation of the freight market. Those operating in the industry have had to be nimble and respond to the changes in the supply chain infrastructure. "One thing is certain: As long as trade is being used as a negotiating tool, companies with supply chains will struggle to keep costs manageable," said Henry Byers, market expert on international freight forwarding and maritime at FreightWaves, in his June analysis.

The anecdotal evidence of *fewer* U.S. gulf cargoes heading for China is an indicator of this, Sand explained. "Once disrupted, the damage to the trade lanes is done. New trade lanes have occurred, and new partnerships deals are made for future flow of goods. Global economics have also changed since the start of the trade war, so it's all different. Trust is broken."

U.S. Against the World

While the trade war predominantly impacts the United States and China, its tremendous size and scope has initiated multiple other trade wars, which cannot be ignored. This map illustrates the countries that have hit back at the United States with retaliatory tariffs of their own.

U.S. Against the World

Source: Marine Money International

The collective impact of this multifront trade war and the truth behind the disjointed flow of U.S. exports is something that cannot be disproven—the movement of commodities and products tells the truth. This tangible trade is also being verified in the earnings reports of companies that operate all around the world.

"In the 2019 second-quarter reportings of 451 companies, 84 (or 19 percent) came up short of expectations," explained Nick Raich, CEO of the Earnings Scout. "Of those companies missing on earnings, 68 percent mentioned tariffs and/or trade in either their earnings reports or subsequent conference calls afterward. The sectors with the most mentions of tariffs? Energy, materials, industrials, and technology."

Raich said that according to their research the escalation of the trade war has reduced 2019 S&P 500's earnings by 2.1 percent, and additional tariffs and/or cuts in capital spending could impact earnings even more. "If the trade war escalates into the fall, 2020 earning per share estimates are highly likely to get reduced by even a greater amount later in 2019."

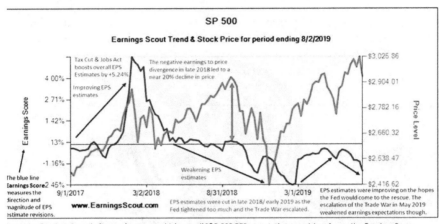

On the small-business side, the impact depends on the materials sourced, but the one thing businesses of all sizes have in common is the impact the uncertainty can have on their planning. "Small businesses are cautious about the issue of tariffs," says Martin Mucci, Paychex president and CEO. "However, our research shows that the majority of small businesses are not being affected. Of those that are, their owners cite increased costs as the greatest impact, which is understandable—small businesses generally have less leverage to change suppliers or pass new costs along to customers."

Manufacturers reported in the Federal Reserve Bank of Boston Beige Book that "tariffs and foreign retaliation had weakened demand for their products," and "investment demand had slowed because firms were delaying capital expenditure plans."[122]

Mark Zandi, chief economist at Moody's Analytics, warned that the longer the trade war continues on, the less likely it is trade flows will return to what they were prior to the war. "This may already be the case as American companies have already begun shifting their sourcing and supply chains, and moving them back to where they were may be too costly," he explained. "Global trading volumes may also be lower longer-run, as the U.S. and China disengage their economies. These are the two largest trading nations in the world, and if they aren't doing as much business with each other, then global trade will be diminished."

Boomerang Effect

The flow of trade has forecast for months the massive drop-off in U.S. exports and the impact the trade war has had on industries like agriculture in the U.S. The trickle-down impact of this trade war and the cooling of domestic demand for manufacturing were the major themes in the August 2019 survey by the Institute for Supply Management. For the first time since 2016, the survey highlighting manufacturing production, demand, and sales showed a drop to 49.1 percent in August from 51.2 percent in July. Steeper declines were also recorded in the indexes for employment (47.4%) and new export orders (43.3%). The companies that participated in the survey cited the shrinking of export orders as a result of the trade dispute, as well as the mounting challenges they face in moving supply chains out of China to avoid the tariffs.

"The U.S. trade war with the world has blown open a great big hole in manufacturers' confidence," Chris Rupkey, chief financial economist at MUFG Union Bank, wrote. "The manufacturing sector has officially turned down and is falling for the first time this year as the China tariffs and slowdown in exports have really started to bite."

The boomerang of the tariff slap has officially smacked back.

In the face of the undeniable facts, President Trump doubled down on the narrative of the United States winning the trade war and his go-it-alone approach.

---

[122]   Federal Reserve Bank of Boston Beige Book, July 17, 2019

Donald J. Trump ✅
@realDonaldTrump

For all of the "geniuses" out there, many who have been in other administrations and "taken to the cleaners" by China, that want me to get together with the EU and others to go after China Trade practices remember, the EU & all treat us VERY unfairly on Trade also. Will change!

9:33 AM · Sep 3, 2019 · Twitter for iPhone

The Pinch

Remember what U.S. Customs and Border Patrol said about who pays the tariffs. "The importer of record (company) is the entity that is liable and pays for the tariffs in full. That means 100 percent of all commodity lines coming into the U.S. are paid for by the U.S. importer. The importer is liable to pay that reported amount." This is how the truth of free trade and the flow of containers prevails over the rhetoric.

In a JPMorgan report in August, analyst Dubravoko Lakos-Bujas predicted the 10 percent implemented would cost the average American family between $600 to $1,000 per year, which would eat away most of the $1,300 tax break they received in tax reform.[123]

Where Do We Go From Here?

With a long list of additional tariffs in the queue, ready to be slapped on more trading partners, the bluster of new threats and promises in the trade negotiations is to be expected. There should be no surprise. Tariffs are the Trump administration's way of getting a country's attention in order to negotiate. Hit them in their pocketbook so they take a seat at the table. In the end, trade negotiations should be measured by the *actions* of those participating in the discussions. Good faith should have a track record of real results.

"China has made small purchases in faith, but for us to make up for the trade we have lost with them, we need to have a 92 percent market share with every country that is importing soybeans right now," said Monte Peterson, a soybean

---

[123] Dubravoko Lakos-Bujas, "Impact From the Latest Round of Tariffs," JP Morgan, August 16, 2019

farmer from North Dakota and the director of the American Soybean Association and the U.S. Soybean Export Council (USSEC). "Even though shipments from the Pacific Northwest to China are lagging by 53 percent, they are still nine times the business than the second largest market for the PNW, which is Taiwan."

When you think of infrastructure, you traditionally think of bridges, roads, and tunnels. For the agriculture industry, plowing land is considered building infrastructure. "The thing I am most concerned about is that our number one competitor, Brazil, is pursuing greater volume of production, and they are clearing ground to grow more bushels, thousands of acres," said Derek Haigwood, chairman of the U.S. Soybean Export Council and a soybean farmer from Arkansas. "Acreage stays forever, it never goes back. Even if the trade war is solved tomorrow, those acres are there *forever*."

Brazil's soybean acreage augmentation to supply more soybeans to China as well as China's relocation of Chinese farmers to Russia to plant soybean crops are just two examples of the acreage expansion that in the end replaces U.S. acreage.

The ongoing trade war has also drained the U.S.-China energy relationship. In July, which is traditionally the strongest month for the Chinese import of U.S. crude, China imported approximately 261,000 barrels per day (bpd), which is below the 344,000 bpd rate for the first six months of the year.[124] Crude, remember, at that time was not on China's retaliatory tariff list (crude was added to China's tariff list on September 1). The July pullback in oil was just another piece of trade plumbing stopped up because of the trade war. LNG, on the other hand, was already on the tariff list. LNG, which has been a key part in the U.S. energy independence story, is all but dead in China. Since Chinese entities signed 37 major deals with U.S. firms (including two LNG deals) in early November 2017, the LNG trade to China has essentially died.

The lack of China's trade promised within the trade negotiations is highlighted by the flow of trade. If discussions were *really* progressing, U.S. exports to China would be ticking *up*, not down. The trade gap should be *narrowing*, not expanding. The beauty of measuring trade negotiations by the volumes of goods being transported through the plumbing of maritime is that it is not political. There is no posturing or spin. The data speaks for itself. Is a country buying like it promised? Are products or commodities being silently boycotted? Did the

---

[124] Clyde Russell, "For China, U.S. Soybeans Are Small Fry; Crude, LNG, Coal Are the Main Game," Reuters, July 30, 2019

country in question find new countries to trade with, in lieu of the country it is in negotiations with? The answers to those questions, and the truth of a trading partner's good will, are in the trade data. The winners and losers of the trade war are also in that data.

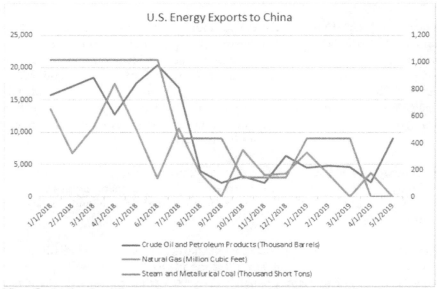

Note: *Crude oil and petroleum products and natural gas on left axis, coal on right axis*
Source: U.S. Energy Information Administration

Maritime is agnostic, and shipping will always be nimble enough to move the flow of trade. It's the job of the industry. The traditional way of trade negotiation may have changed, but the business of the sea has not. For the flow of trade to move in today's trade war, new currents have been created as a result of the tsunami of tariffs. In the end, the interconnectedness of trade will always find a way to work.

In an email to clients on October 16, 2019, BIMCO chief shipping analyst Peter Sand warned, "Container shipping is a servant to the consumption of the advanced economies and a slowdown in GDP growth of these economies will lead to lower container shipping demand in the foreseeable future."

"Major container carriers have blanked sailings, hoping to lift freight rates, but without any significant improvement. Although, to everyone's surprise, the Far East-Europe trade lane is up 4.6 percent in accumulated volumes year-over-year, indicating that tariffed goods headed for the U.S. might be transhipped through Europe to circumvent the American tariff wall."

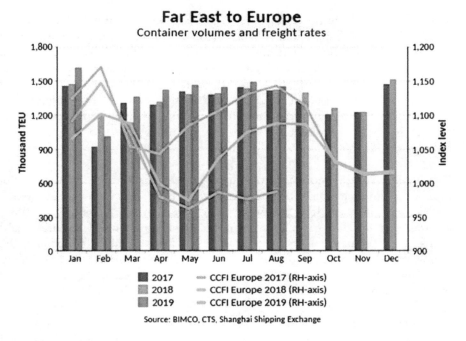

Far East to Europe
Container volumes and freight rates

Source: BIMCO, CTS, Shanghai Shipping Exchange

These new trade flows have been soldered by the ingenuity of companies altering their strategies to grow or maintain their businesses. In the face of accusations of being "untrustworthy trading partners," American CEOs, farmers, and entrepreneurs are rising above, creating new relationships and finding new markets to move their products to. These new customers may not fill the huge bucket China once filled, but some volume is better than none.

The competitiveness of world trade has also been highlighted during this trade war, with the likes of Canada, Brazil, and Vietnam aggressively tapping into the opportunities the trade war has created. This is how free trade prevails, by navigating the blustery winds of rhetoric and tariffs. Trade may have become a sharp political weapon, but remember: Containers and tankers don't lie.

EPILOGUE

In this new book authored by Lori Ann LaRocco and initiated by Marine Money, the reader finds a well-substantiated account of the negative impact of trade wars on trade flows. The author, a seasoned business journalist, analyzed this instance of trade war through different angles, looking in particular at changes in volumes and the use of containers, in which the bulk of internationally traded goods are transported. With a good understanding of the geopolitics and geoeconomics of international trade, the author focuses on two main and closely interrelated actors turned to protagonists: the United States and China.

The book marries a good analysis based on extensive data with a skillful journalistic investigation, pushing the reader to avidly follow the exciting modern saga of the trade war between these two giants. Looking at trade flows and mutual trade patterns in aluminum and steel, agriculture, and energy, and then examining maritime trade logistics at U.S. ports and of containers, the author shows the deterioration in trade flows between these two economies, which have become so intertwined through trade and finance in a matter of only two and a half decades.

Such deterioration is a further manifestation of serious negative developments in the world trade system, which was already drifting away from a multilateral regime toward a spaghetti bowl panoply of bilateral trade accords prone to constant renegotiations. The author checks the proclaimed intentions against the reality, and concludes that the U.S. trade policies are more self-defeating than they are protecting of American producers and consumers. While the aim is to rebalance trade and decrease the ballooning U.S. trade deficit with China, the evidence shows that the trade war is not decreasing the trade deficit but rather disproportionately hitting American exporters to Chinese markets, for example in the areas of agriculture and energy.

But more importantly, the book reminds us of how dangerous for the world economy and security the continuing confrontation between such economic giants so deeply intertwined in the area of mutual trade and finance could be. It is warning us that the trade war initiated by the U.S. and reciprocated by China may degenerate into a global economic crisis and dangerous geopolitical conflicts. Interestingly, the author quotes Chair of the Federal Reserve Jerome Powell saying diplomatically but at the same time quite powerfully at the last Jackson Hole conference, "Trade policy uncertainty seems to be playing a role in the global slowdown and in weak manufacturing and capital spending in the United States."

The rule-based multilateral trading system, together with technological advances, standardization, and logistics, was among the driving forces behind the expansion of global trade and the opening up of national economies, i.e., international trade's increasing share of GDP. In 1960, trade as a share of the world's GDP stood at 24 percent; today it has reached almost 60 percent. However, after the crisis of the Doha round of negotiations, the stalemate of the multilateral trade regime brought about a proliferation of bilateral and regional trade agreements and increasing contradictions between trading partners.

Nevertheless, even after Doha, trade between the U.S. and China continued its rapid expansion. One of the reasons for the increasing linkages between them was the massive investment by U.S. corporations into the productive manufacturing sector of China, the latter providing a vast pool of low-cost and skillful labor and a potentially huge market. The increase in Chinese export potential, apart from the participation in global supply chains of investing in transnational corporations, was also a result of active government policies supporting local enterprises through the instruments of trade, fiscal and financial incentives, and subsidies, permitting Chinese exporters to dramatically increase their presence in the U.S., European, and other foreign markets. Delocalization and a decreasing share of manufacturing in the U.S. and other developed countries affected the middle classes in those countries and brought about a political backlash. In the case of the U.S., this is now becoming dangerous for the world economy by leading to global trade wars.

It is true that during this period the relationship between the two countries in terms of the United States' acceptance of China's economic policies was quite problematic. The Chinese government was criticized not only for offering subsidies to Chinese exporters to the U.S. markets but also for excessive demands on the transfer of technologies by U.S. investors in China, which was perceived as violating intellectual property rights. However, those issues should not be addressed with a trade war, but rather by working out differences and searching for mutually acceptable solutions. At the same time, the World Trade Organization (WTO) rules are still relevant and can be applied in a genuine attempt to overcome differences. Maybe China is perceived as a geopolitical competitor, but hitting a competitor can also be self-defeating. A much better approach is for the countries to consider each other as international trade and investment partners and discuss differences in a spirit of building up a more sustainable model for the world economy.

Commentators on the global economic crisis of 2008 blamed financial speculation, especially the bubble of mortgage derivatives and deregulation of financial markets, as its main cause. Some of them brought up world trade as an example of a multilateral rule-based system playing a positive role and taming excesses in the world economy. This time, the possibility of a global crisis comes from a direct attack on this multilateral rule-based trading system, through tariff wars and escalations and the outright cancellation of trade contracts between the two biggest economies of the world.

In conclusion, the negative impacts of the trade war are threefold. First, there is the direct impact on trade flows. While there are winners and losers, the total net impact on global trade is negative. It is not a zero-sum game, as some want us to believe. Research by the United Nations Conference on Trade and Development (UNCTAD) has shown that the regions most negatively affected are North America and East Asia, especially for trade in intermediate manufactured goods. UNCTAD shows how shipping is detrimentally affected as seaborne trade continues to grow at a lower rate than the commercial fleet.

Secondly, there is the negative impact on investment. Uncertainty is the worst enemy of investment, as it increases risks and could jeopardize the minimum return on investment that an investor requires. And the uncertainty associated with trade wars has already had a negative impact on foreign direct investment as measured in the latest World Investment Report of UNCTAD. This decline does not bode well for the long-term prospects of international trade and global value chains.

Finally, the accompanying politics of the tariff wars have a negative bearing on the multilateral trading system as they are weakening the functioning of the WTO. As the large countries turn to bilateral measures, why should others abide by the global rules? And if the dispute settlement mechanism of the WTO is further weakened by not filling vacant positions, the functioning of the entire system is jeopardized.

Lori Ann LaRocco's book also hints at one of the underlying causes of the trade wars. She writes: "In a world where diplomacy and trade negotiations play out in real time on social media, it is understandable how the global markets could move so suddenly over a 280-character tweet. This is the first time in history that the world can be a spectator to this diplomatic process." Followers and opponents of President Donald Trump are increasingly reading and liking and retweeting within their own echo chambers of opinions. The result of this trend is a polarization of political opinions, where negotiations and compromise become the exception rather than the rule.

The deviation of trade flows toward other destinations, while absorbing a part of the shock, cannot replace the importance of stable relationships based on the deep interdependence between the United States and China which now, instead of playing the role of anchors, are absorbed by their conflict and thus swinging the ship of the world economy. It is time to come back to common sense and start searching for solutions for a sustainable future, as the increasing dichotomy between announced intentions and negative developments so ably shown in this book could lead to a dangerous if not disastrous alternative.

Dr. Rouben Indjikian, *former senior official at UNCTAD, is professor of International Trade and Finance at Webster University Geneva*

Dr. Jan Hoffmann, *Chief of Trade Logistics Branch, Division on Technology and Logistics, at UNCTAD*

AFTERWORD

For millennia, the principal way in which trade occurred between continents was shipping. Ships could carry more cargo more quickly and more efficiently than land transportation.

Indeed, America was "discovered" by Christopher Columbus as he searched for a quicker way (than around the Horn of Africa) to transport goods to and from India and Asia.

Technology has obviously evolved considerably since Columbus's day, and air transportation is now frequently used to convey products between continents. But shipping is still the major way that goods are shipped between continents.

For that reason, an astute analysis of shipping activities around the world can lead to an amazingly accurate picture of what is occurring in global trade, i.e., who is shipping what to whom, whether shipping is increasing or decreasing, and how trade patterns are evolving and changing.

And such a picture can be valuable in assessing economic patterns and in forecasting economic events.

Lori Ann LaRocco has done a real favor for those who follow economic patterns and predict economic events by carefully analyzing shipping patterns and reminding everyone that shipping is really the key indicator in global trade.

Her analysis of what is currently occurring—in part because of changing trade rules and constraints—provides real insights into the current global economy, regardless of your view of the merits of any particular government policy.

So readers should take away from this book three key ideas:

1. Shipping patterns still provide—many years after Columbus—the best way to understand what is occurring in global trade. And the more exhaustive the analysis, the more insights will be gained about global trade.

2. Global trade is still one of the essential keys to understanding global economic patterns.

3. Lori Ann LaRocco has provided a first class analysis of current shipping patterns and their implications for global trade. By doing so, she has given us a book that is a must-read for any student of global trade (and the global economy).

David M. Rubenstein, *The Carlyle Group Co-Founder, Co-Executive Chairman*

ACKNOWLEDGEMENTS

As a journalist who covers business news and maritime, this project was a personal one for me. The daily happenings of trade and the impact it has on Americans both financially and emotionally needed to be told. Only part of the story was out there. My husband, Michael, and children, Nicholas, Declan, and Abby, understood how important this project was for me and stood by me 100 percent. I love you all very much, and my heart overflows with gratitude. Nick, Declan, Abby—no matter how many books I write, you three will be my greatest accomplishment. We are put on this earth to make a difference and to leave it a little better than when we came in. You are well on your way to carving an amazing path. You all make me proud. Samantha Baietti, thank you for being my barometer outside of the business world and reading the book. Your feedback was invaluable.

Thank you to Dan Colarusso, Lacy O'Toole, Brian Steel, and Mark Hoffman at CNBC for giving me the nod in pursuing this project. Many thanks to Jim Lawrence for listening to my book idea and letting me run with it. To the amazing women of Marine Money, without whom this project never would have come together—Molly, Alexa, and Julia: Molly, you are a transcribing machine!! I don't know how you did it all! Alexa, thank you for your editorial touch. Julia, thanks for keeping everyone on track! Thank you for everything!!

To all my contacts who provided their expertise in telling this story: Your data and analysis were invaluable. Without your crucial information, the points made in this book would have been reduced to more rhetoric. This blustery trade war does not need any more of that!

Kevin Book, thank you for your no-nonsense, give-it-to-me-straight comments. I appreciated the direction, and you made me better. Peter Sand, thank you for your maritime insight. BIMCO really is a gem in the world of maritime data. You and your team laid out the truth in the flow of trade. Steve Ferreira, thank you for your mastery in navigating the bills of lading and uncovering some of the best data sets on trade flow. I always enjoy our conversations and the insight you bring. Simply amazing.

Intermodal powerhouses FTR and FreightWaves, your data and analysis were invaluable. The truth in the flow of the containers and cargo moving within the United States further emphasized the impact of the trade war. Henry Byers, Seth Teeters, thank you for all your hard work and coordination.

Many thanks and deep appreciation to Mario Cordero, the Port of Long Beach staff, Chris Lytle, the Port of Oakland staff, and Gene Seroka, Phil Sanfeld, and the amazing data team at the Port of Los Angeles. By opening the ports to the readers of this book and telling them your story, you provided them with insight and knowledge they could not get anywhere else.

Finally, my deepest and warmest appreciation to those who had the courage to share their personal stories on the challenges and opportunities this trade war has created for them. This trade war is not a simple black-and-white story of "winning" and "losing." There are many shades of gray, and it's those shades of gray that provide the true color and full context to this historic event. Mike Bless, Barry Zekelman, Tom Lix, Jeff Tucker, Cindy Brown, and Christopher Gibbs—by sharing your business experiences I believe you have provided the balance this book needed to show the challenges and opportunities facing the various industries. Thank you.

ABOUT THE AUTHOR

Lori Ann LaRocco is senior editor of guests for CNBC business news. She coordinates high-profile interviews in business and politics, as well as special multimillion dollar on-location productions for all shows on the network. Her specialty is in politics, working with titans of industry. LaRocco is the author of *Dynasties of the Sea, Part 2: The Untold Stories of the Postwar Shipping Pioneers* (Marine Money, Inc., 2018), *Opportunity Knocking* (Agate Publishing, 2014), *Dynasties of the Sea: The Shipowners and Financiers Who Expanded the Era of Free Trade* (Marine Money, Inc., 2012), and *Thriving in the New Economy: Lessons from Today's Top Business Minds* (Wiley, 2010).

LaRocco has been working at CNBC since 2000. Her track record has garnered trust and respect from Wall Street to Washington. By establishing relationships with some of the best in business, LaRocco has been the first to learn of business deals in the billions of dollars, enabling CNBC to break the news.

Prior to joining CNBC, LaRocco was an anchor, reporter, and assignment editor in various local news markets around the country.

GLOSSARY

The Baltic and International Maritime Council (BIMCO) – A nongovernmental organization and the world's largest international shipping organization. Its shipowner members control roughly 65 percent of the world's available tonnage. Other members include managers, brokers, and agents across 120 countries.

Basis Point – A basis point is 1/100 of 1 percent, or 0.01 percent. It is frequently used to describe the percentage change in the value or rate of a financial instrument.

Belt and Road Initiative (BRI) – A global infrastructure program first announced in 2013 by Chinese President Xi Jinping, designed to rework international trade networks to place China as the central hub for global trade. It consists of land and maritime transportation infrastructure investments in 152 countries across the Americas, Asia, Europe, Africa, and the Middle East with a targeted date of completion in 2049.

Break Bulk – A form of transporting cargoes that cannot be easily packaged in standardized cargo containers (see Containerization, Intermodal System) and are individually loaded into cargo holds. These cargoes are usually packaged in bags, crates, drums, barrels, etc. While requiring more manpower to move cargo than the Intermodal System, it needs far fewer facilities to discharge cargo, making it popular in less developed ports.

British Thermal Unit (BTU) – The amount of energy required to heat one pound of water by one degree at sea level.

Bulk Carrier – A ship designed to carry unpackaged dry cargoes such as ore or grain.

Bumper Crop – An unusually bountiful harvest. This can become an issue when there is insufficient storage capacity for the crop.

Capital – The financial and physical assets of a company.

Container Ships – Ships designed to carry containers stacked in cargo holds and/or on deck. Cargo capacity is measured in TEUs and typically ranges from 100–18,000 TEU capacity.

Containerization – A system of intermodal freight transportation utilizing standardized shipping containers. Containers are most frequently found in 20- and 40-foot lengths, although larger sizes are available. Finished products, such as electronics or home products, are usually carried within containers, with some containers occasionally being fitted with tanks to transport small amounts of liquid cargoes. The containerization system was developed by Malcolm McLean, an American trucker, in the 1950s.

Cost, Insurance, and Freight (CIF) – An expense paid by a seller to cover the costs, insurance, and freight against possible losses/damages to the buyer's order while in transit to the export port specified in the sales contract. This also covers the expense of additional paperwork, customs, inspections, or reroutings. The buyer only becomes responsible for costs after the freight is unloaded.

Crude Steel – Steel in its first solid state after melting that can be sold as is or further refined. It usually takes the form of ingots, slabs, billets, or liquid steel for casting.

Deadweight Ton (DWT) – The carrying capacity of a ship, including bunkers, water, stores, and cargo, measured in metric tons.

Department of Commerce – A department of the executive branch of the U.S. government concerned with promoting economic growth, gathering economic and demographic data to aid businesses and federal and local governments in decision-making, and setting industrial standards.

Drayage – The transportation of goods over a short distance; usually constitutes a small part of a larger chain of transportation.

Dry Bulk – Unpackaged solid cargoes such as iron ore, grain, or scrap metal; contrast to containerized, bagged, or palletized cargo.

Dumping – The act of a foreign nation or company flooding the local economy with a product or products that are cheaper than what can be produced and sold domestically.

European Union (E.U.) – A confederation of 28 European Countries: Austria, Belgium, Bulgaria, Croatia, Cyprus, Czech Republic, Denmark, Estonia, Finland, France, Germany, Greece, Hungary, Ireland, Italy, Latvia, Lithuania, Luxembourg, Malta, The Netherlands, Poland, Portugal, Romania, Slovakia, Slovenia, Spain, Sweden, and the U.K. The E.U. has its own supranational government and is a single market. Nineteen E.U. members—Austria, Belgium, Cyprus, Estonia, Finland, France, Germany, Greece, Ireland, Italy, Latvia, Lithuania, Luxembourg, Malta, the Netherlands, Portugal, Slovakia, Slovenia, and Spain—use the euro, a common currency that is accepted in many places in the E.U. that haven't adopted the euro and nations bordering the E.U.

Federal Information Security Modernization Act of 2014 (FISMA) – Codifies the Department of Homeland Security's role in administering the implementation of information security policies for federal Executive Branch

170

civilian agencies, overseeing agencies' compliance with those policies, and assisting OMB in developing those policies.

Fixed Asset Investment – The purchasing of physical assets such as machinery, land, buildings, vehicles, etc.

Flat Products – Slabs, hot- or cold-rolled coil, coated steel products, tinplate, and heavy plate steel products, as well as products frequently used in automotive, heavy machinery, pipes, tubes, construction, etc.

Foreign Direct Investment (FDI) – A form of investment that places the controlling interest of a company in a foreign entity.

Free Alongside Ship (FAS) – The seller's price quote for the goods, including delivery charges at the contractually specified port. The seller will handle the cost of wharfage and clear the goods for exporting; the buyer is responsible for the cost to load, transport, and insure the cargo.

Front-Loading – A method of attempting to avoid upcoming tariffs by increasing production speed and/or decreasing transportation time.

Fungible – Used to describe commodities or goods that can replace an equal amount of another commodity or good without affecting value or quality. For example, two barrels of the same classification of fuel are fungible goods, while a barrel of ultra-low-sulphur marine gas oil and a barrel of heavy fuel oil are not fungible goods.

G-20 – An international forum of Australia, Argentina, Brazil, Canada, China, France, Germany, India, Indonesia, Italy, Japan, Mexico, Russia, Saudi Arabia, South Africa, South Korea, Turkey, the U.K., the U.S., the E.U., the Chairman of the International Monetary Fund, the International Monetary and Financial Committee, the President of the World Bank, and the Development Assistance Committee. The G-20 was founded in 1999 to coordinate global economic policy.

G-7 – An international intergovernmental organization consisting of the seven largest "advanced economies" as described by the International Monetary Fund: Canada, France, Germany, Italy, Japan, the U.K., and the United States. The purpose of the organization is to give political leaders a chance to meet annually to discuss and exchange ideas on topics such as energy and the global economy. It was known as the G-8 until Russia was suspended over the annexation of Crimean Peninsula in 2014.

Gross Domestic Product (GDP) – The value of goods and services produced within a country.

Gulf Cooperation Council (GCC) – A regional intergovernmental political and economic union consisting of Saudi Arabia, Kuwait, the UAE, Qatar, Bahrain, and Oman. The purpose is to form a customs union to create a common market and currency in the region. Additional goals include creating economic regulations, joint scientific ventures, and a unified military.

Harmonized System (HS) Code 1201 – The Harmonized System is the internationally standardized system to classify products for trade; 1201 is the heading code for soybeans.

Import Penetration – The proportion of the market for a particular good/product that is supplied by imports.

Intellectual Property – An invention, idea, or work resulting from creativity to which one has rights and for which one may apply for patents, copyrights, trademarks, etc.

Intellectual Property Theft – The act of robbing an entity of its ideas, inventions, or creative expression. This includes trade secrets, proprietary products, software, and patents.

Intermodal System – A form of transporting freight in standardized containers (see Containerization) through various forms of transportation (ship, truck, rail). Because the cargo is stored within standardized containers, the individual pieces of cargo don't need to be individually unpacked and repacked when changing forms of transportation (see Break Bulk).

International Emergency Economic Powers Act (IEEPA) – A U.S. federal law enacted in 1977 that allows the United States president to regulate international commerce should a national emergency be declared in response to a threat to the U.S. that originated at least partially outside the United States.

International Monetary Fund (IMF) – An organization headquartered in Washington, D.C., formed in 1944 to encourage global monetary cooperation, secure financial stability, promote high employment rates and sustainable economic growth, and reduce poverty across its 189 member nations.

International Trade Commission (ITC) – An independent and bipartisan federal agency that provides trade expertise to the legislative and executive branches of the U.S. government.

Liquified Natural Gas (LNG) – Natural gas that has been converted from a gaseous state to a liquid state by chilling it between -120 and -170°C. By liquifying it, it becomes 600 times denser than its gaseous state and allows it to be economically transported or used as a transportation fuel.

Metallurgical Coal – A grade of coal used in making coke, the primary fuel and reactant in blast furnaces used in steelmaking. The demand for metallurgical coal is tied to the demand for steel.

Monetary/Quantitative Easing – A strategy that a central bank can use to increase the supply of money in a nation's economy. This is accomplished by the central bank's purchasing of securities when interest rates are near zero percent.

National Retail Federation (NRF) – The world's largest retail trade association, consisting of department stores, chain restaurants, grocery stores, independent retailers, internet retailers, discount and catalogue stores, etc.

Natural Gas – A hydrocarbon mixture of primarily methane formed from decomposing organic matter under intense heat and pressure over the span of millions of years. At standard pressure and room temperature, it is a colorless gas. Odorizers are added to natural gas to help detect gas leaks.

North American Free Trade Agreement (NAFTA) – A 1993 agreement between the United States, Canada, and Mexico to eliminate tariffs between the signatories. Donald Trump sought to renegotiate after taking office, leading to the creation of the United States–Mexico–Canada Agreement (USMCA) in 2018. NAFTA will remain in effect until each signatory's legislature ratifies the USMCA.

Organization for Economic Cooperation and Development (OECD) – An intergovernmental organization comprised of 36 member countries, founded in 1961 to stimulate economic progress and global trade.

Panamax – The largest ship size that can fit through the old Panama Canal locks, typically 290 meters by 32 meters with a laden draft of 12 meters and air draft of 57 meters. These ships can carry 60,000–100,000 DWT, or 5,000 TEU.

Port Share – The percentage of a nation's total TEU for the year received by a particular port.

Price Premium – The difference between a product's selling price and its benchmark price, represented as a percentage.

Primary Aluminum – Aluminum that is created by refining ore (Bauxite) rather than recycling aluminum scrap.

Purchasing Manufacturer's Index (PMI) – An index designed to show trends in the manufacturing and service sectors in terms of growth or contraction.

Section 232 of the Trade Expansion Act of 1962 – Authorizes the president of the United States to adjust the imports of goods and materials from foreign nations using tariffs if the quantity or circumstance of those imports threatens national security.

Section 304 of the Trade Act of 1974 – Enacted in 1975, the Trade Act of 1974 was designed to help transition workers into other industries and increase competitiveness of U.S. industries by giving the president broad authority to fight against unfair or injurious foreign trade practices; Section 304 outlines the duties of the U.S. Trade Representative to determine if the rights of the U.S. under its trade agreements are being denied and what actions should be subsequently taken.

Suezmax – The largest ship size that can fit through the Suez Canal, usually in reference to tankers. There is no length restriction for ships passing through the Suez Canal, but they cannot exceed a maximum beam of 77 meters, maximum draft of 20.1 meters, and maximum air draft of 68 meters.

Supramax/Handymax – A variety of Handysize Dry Bulk vessels carrying between 40,000–59,999 DWT.

Tanker – A ship designed to carry liquid cargoes in bulk. Frequently carries cargoes such as crude oil, gasoline and other refined oil products, vegetable oils, fruit juice, fresh water, etc. Ships can be designed to carry a single type of cargo or a variety of cargoes.

Technology Transfers – The act of transferring technology owned or held by a government, company, university, etc. to another organization.

Trans-Pacific Partnership (TPP) – A defunct trade agreement between Australia, Brunei, Canada, Chile, Japan, Malaysia, Mexico, New Zealand, Peru, Singapore, the United States, and Vietnam. The U.S. signed in early 2016 but withdrew its signature three days into the Trump administration. The remaining nations formed a separate agreement.

Truck Turn Time – The elapsed time between a truck arriving in the queue, passing through the entry gate and all checkpoints, and exiting the gate and the final checkpoints.

Twenty-foot Equivalent Unit (TEU) – A generalized unit of measurement of the cargo capacity of a vehicle based on the capacity of a standard 20-foot shipping container, with one TEU equaling the capacity to carry one 20-foot shipping container.

United States–Mexico–Canada Agreement (USMCA) – The current iteration of NAFTA that was renegotiated from 2017–2018. Among other facets of the agreement, it's been lauded for its adjustment of automotive rules of origin, new digital trade measures, and increased trade secret protections, while being condemned for its lack of enforceable labor standards, lack of dispute resolution mechanisms, and expansion of patent length for biological substances, thus preventing cheaper generic medicines from entering the U.S. market.

United States Trade Representative (USTR) – A U.S. governmental agency responsible for conducting trade negotiations and coordinating, developing, and recommending U.S. trade policy to the president of the United States. (See Section 304 of the Trade Act of 1974.)

Very Large Crude Carrier (VLCC) – A variety of tanker designed to carry between 160,000 and 319,999 DWT, roughly equivalent to 2,000,000 barrels of oil (10 percent of the U.S.'s daily consumption of oil).

World Trade Organization (WTO) – An international organization with 164 member countries (as of July 29, 2016), committed to reducing barriers to international trade of goods, services, and intellectual property. It replaced the General Agreement on Trade and Tariffs (GATT) in 1995.

Year-over-Year (YoY) – A type of financial analysis that shows the change in financial instruments from one period of time in a year to the same period of time in the next year.

Year-to-Date (YTD) – A period of time that can begin at either the beginning of the calendar year or the beginning of the fiscal year and ends at the present day.

MARINE MONEY, INC.

CPSIA information can be obtained
at www.ICGtesting.com
Printed in the USA
BVHW010354201119
564362BV00003B/4/P